"With any hot issue facing Catholics—and certainly when pondering papal authority and its exercise and abuse—it's highly advisable to check with Peter Kwasniewski before rushing to your own conclusion. I find that he always adds additional protein, at a minimum, and often gives you a menu for the entire discussion. This work, in companion volumes, provides the latter."

—**ROGER MCCAFFREY**, Editor, *The Traditionalist*

"Avoiding extremes of 'papolatry' and antipapalism, Dr. Kwasniewski's analysis brings sorely needed balance to contemporary discussions about the role of the papacy in the Church. The first volume helps Catholics rediscover an integrated vision of the office of the pope, not as an autocratic arbiter over the faith but as the servant and defender of Tradition; the second builds up the author's case by concrete reference to the past decade."

—**PHILLIP CAMPBELL**, author of the *Story of Civilization* series

"In hysterical times such as our own, nothing is more important in Church and State than that sane voices be raised and heard. In a period when we are all expected to have immediate opinions on every topic under the sun—no matter how ignorant we may be in this or that area—the result is often a similarly hysterical internal turmoil. Nowhere is this truer than in the Catholic Church under the current pontificate. In the first volume of this work, Dr. Kwasniewski guides us with a sure and sane hand through two millennia of papal history and theology in order to bring us to an accurate understanding of the papacy, showing it to be neither a mere human institution nor another oracle at Delphi. In the second volume he applies these hard-won principles to the various bizarre episodes of the current pontificate. Above all, he shows us how Catholics ought to react to the current crisis in the Church: keeping their eyes on the prize of their eternal salvation. We owe him an enormous debt."

—**CHARLES COULOMBE**, author of *Vicars of Christ: A History of the Popes*

"Dr. Kwasniewski offers an essential resource for coping with the great mystery of our times: how can recent popes, and especially Francis, do so much harm to the Mystical Body of Christ? The answer is not a simple one because we are dealing with a mystery. Avoiding both sophistry and oversimplification, Kwasniewski navigates the safe ground of history and Catholic tradition to build a framework in which we can attempt to live with the mystery until Our Lord decides to heal this crisis."

—**BRIAN M. MCCALL**, Editor-in-Chief, *Catholic Family News*

"In this timely two-volume collection of essays and articles, Peter Kwasniewski gets to grips with the overwhelming scandal facing us today: a Pope who day by day is betraying his divine office and leading the faithful into heresy. It is important to keep the enormity of this before the Church, and to show how it has been made possible by an exaggerated adulation of the person of the reigning Pontiff."

—**HENRY SIRE**, author of *The Dictator Pope*

"Dr. Kwasniewski helps the reader living through the current unprecedented Church crisis to leave behind a widespread and unhealthy hyperpapalism and move on to a Catholic perception of the papacy and its place in the Church. He quotes saintly authorities showing that already back in the thirteenth and fourteenth centuries there was a clear knowledge of the pope being just the 'vicar,' the representative of Christ: he does not supplant Jesus Christ, and he therefore must not change the faith but preserve, clarify, and amplify it—like a good photographer who works on his pictures: he does not change the motifs on it, but increases the contrast and brightens the colors. It is perfectly Catholic to adhere to the teaching of the Church, even when bishops and the pope try to alter it. For, as St. Vincent of Lérins insisted, 'All possible care must be taken that we hold that faith which has been believed everywhere, always, by all.'"

—**MONIKA RHEINSCHMITT**, President, *Pro Missa Tridentina*

THE ROAD FROM HYPERPAPALISM
TO CATHOLICISM

RELATED BOOKS
BY PETER KWASNIEWSKI

Resurgent in the Midst of Crisis
Noble Beauty, Transcendent Holiness
Tradition and Sanity
Reclaiming Our Roman Catholic Birthright
The Holy Bread of Eternal Life
Ministers of Christ
True Obedience in the Church

RELATED BOOKS EDITED
BY PETER KWASNIEWSKI

Are Canonizations Infallible?
From Benedict's Peace to Francis's War
Newman on Worship, Reverence, and Ritual
And Rightly So: Selected Letters and Articles of Neil McCaffrey

The Road from Hyperpapalism to Catholicism

*Rethinking the Papacy
in a Time of
Ecclesial Disintegration*

VOLUME 1
Theological Reflections
on the Rock of the Church

PETER A. KWASNIEWSKI

AROUCA
PRESS

ISBN: 978-1-990685-10-1 (paperback)
ISBN: 978-1-990685-11-8 (hardcover)

Arouca Press
PO Box 55003
Bridgeport PO
Waterloo, ON N2J3G0
Canada
www.aroucapress.com
Send inquiries to info@aroucapress.com

Dedicated to cardinals, bishops, priests, deacons,
religious, and laity around the Catholic world
who have suffered due to the results of
the papal conclave of March 2013
and have prayed earnestly
for divine deliverance
and healing

The Pope is circumscribed by the consciousness of the necessity of making a righteous and beneficent use of the duties attached to his privileges.... He is also circumscribed by the respect due to General Councils and to ancient statutes and customs, by the rights of bishops, by his relation with civil powers, by the traditional mild tone of government indicated by the aim of the institution of the papacy—to "feed"...

Cardinal Joseph Hergenröther

TABLE OF CONTENTS

PREFACE
to the First Volume

ALTHOUGH PRIOR TO 2013 I HAD ALREADY come to see dubious or destructive aspects of the pre-Bergoglian pontificates, I remained to some extent a prisoner of the neo-ultramontanism that flourished among conservative Catholics during the reign of John Paul II,[1] as the first chapter documents to my own embarrassment. It took many shattering and even, in a sense, unbelievable events to force stubborn papalists like myself to dig deeper into the annals of Church history and the resources of Catholic theology. The pontificate of Pope Francis, which has now entered its tenth year, has forced conservative and traditional Catholics to reassess the nature, purpose, and limits of the papal office.

This first volume, *Theological Reflections on the Rock of the Church*, delves into the role of the papacy in Christ's Mystical Body on earth and how we may need to adjust our understanding of that role. It is not only the pope but also and more fundamentally Christ and the Faith entrusted to the Church that are the indestructible rock on which we are to build our lives. The papacy is a limited and temporary office, established to represent Christ the Head of the Church and to carry out those tasks (and only those tasks) for which He instituted it, until He comes again in glory and abolishes all ecclesiastical offices and ceremonies in the blazing glory of the Kingdom of Heaven brought to full perfection. There is a sore need to recalibrate our relationship to a papa*lism* that has, in the last century and a half, overshadowed and distorted the tradition-centered and continuity-protecting papacy as it had been exercised from the time of the early Church, with the reign of St. Pius V as a pinnacle. The companion volume to this one, *Chronological Responses to an Unfolding Pontificate*, by commenting on major events and aspects of the years under Francis, functions effectively as a case-study of the theological principles discussed herein; these principles are both educed from and corroborated by the reality confronting us.

---

1   Well described by Stuart Chessman in his pair of articles: "Ultramontanism: Its Life and Death," *Rorate Caeli*, January 7, 2022; "A Response to José A. Ureta," *Rorate Caeli*, February 22, 2022.

More than would have been the case in times past, today we have to educate ourselves in the Faith and especially in the great monuments of the Faith, which, being universally received over long periods of time and at every level of the Church, are *known* to be certain, authoritative, and reliable—for example, the canons and decrees of the Council of Trent, the *Roman Catechism* published after Trent, and the traditional Latin liturgy with its bimillennial arc of continuity. We can take comfort in the fact that most Catholics for most of history didn't bother with the goings-on in Rome; in many cases they might not even have known the name of the current pope, due to the slow progress of news over vast geographical distances. What, then, did they do? How (one might imagine a papalist of today asking, biting his fingernails) could they ever be—*Catholic*? A simple affair: they held fast to the tried-and-true catechism they had received; they worshiped in the liturgy their forefathers had worshiped in; they prayed as Catholics had prayed for time out of mind and believed what Catholics had always believed.

The content of this book is therefore meant to redound not to bitter lamentation or abrasive hostility but to reassuring consolation and fiery zeal. It reminds the reader that he can *know* what is and what is not Catholic, what looks, sounds, and smells Catholic and what does not, by making energetic use of the mutually reinforcing gifts of faith and reason. These enable us, the sheep of Our Lord Jesus Christ, to listen carefully to the voices emanating from our shepherds and to perceive whether or not the Chief Shepherd's voice is present in theirs.

In the hopeful and spirited words of the great Fr. Roger-Thomas Calmel, O. P. (1914–1975):

> Whatever may be the hypocritical arms placed by modernism in the hands of the episcopal collegialities and even of the Vicar of Christ, tradition will indeed triumph. Solemn baptism, for example, which includes the anathemas against the accursed devil, will not be excluded for long; the tradition of not absolving sins except after individual confession will not be excluded for long; the tradition of the traditional Catholic Mass, Latin and Gregorian, with its language, Canon, and gestures in conformity with the *Roman Missal* of St. Pius V, will soon

be restored to honor; the tradition of the *Catechism of Trent*, or of a manual exactly in conformity with it, will be restored without delay.

On the major points of dogma, morals, the sacraments, the states of life, the perfection to which we are called, the tradition of the Church is known by the members of the Church, whatever their rank. They hold fast to it without a bad conscience, even if the hierarchical guardians of this tradition try to intimidate them or throw them into confusion, even if they persecute them with the bitter refinements of modernist inquisitors. The faithful are very assured that by keeping the tradition they do not cut themselves off from the visible Vicar of Christ. For the visible Vicar of Christ is governed by Christ in such wise that he cannot transmute the tradition of the Church, nor make it fall into oblivion. If by misfortune he should try to do it, either he or his immediate successors will be obliged to proclaim from on high what remains forever living in the Church's memory: the apostolic tradition. The Spouse of Christ stands no chance of losing her memory.[2]

It seems appropriate to add here a few words about Benedict XVI's abdication, a topic that quickly arises in discussions of this sort. I have studied the work of Antonio Socci and Edmund Mazza, and while I find their research intriguing and disturbing in its exposure of rampant theological confusion, none of their arguments has led me to have *moral certainty* that Benedict XVI did not successfully abdicate or intend to abdicate and that Francis, accordingly, is not and never has been the pope. Moreover, I do not believe that the ordinary faithful are competent to adjudicate when God has stripped a pope of the papal office owing to formal heresy. Surely there must be some ecclesiastical process by which stubborn adherence to a particular error or errors, after repeated admonitions, may be ascertained and declared; nor do I regard it as a fatal objection that we currently lack an episcopacy and college of cardinals capable of mounting such a

---

2   "Of the Church and the Pope," *Si Si No No*, January 2006, Reprint #67, www.sspxasia.com/Documents/SiSiNoNo/2006_January/Of_The_Church_And_The_Pope.htm.

challenge. That privation surely does not alter the position of those of us who do not belong to the hierarchy. It is one thing to raise doubts and difficulties about Benedict XVI's abdication and Francis's apparent heresies, leaving the final determination to a future pope or ecumenical council; it is quite another to decide, on one's own, or as part of a small "remnant," that one may cease to recognize as pope the one who is virtually unanimously and universally recognized as pope. The various alternative scenarios that have been put forward suffer from implausibilities and impossibilities at least as great as, if not greater than, the problems to which they are proposed as solutions. For this reason, acknowledging that there are immense gray areas, I have always prayed and continue to pray daily for Pope Francis at Mass and in the Divine Office; I assist at Mass where he is named in the Canon. We are obliged to pray for those placed over us, perhaps most of all when they are disoriented and causing harm. Above all, I beg the Lord to send forth His light and His truth to a Church enfeebled by sin, embittered by scandal, riven by material (if not yet formal) schism.

The essays, lectures, and articles in this book were first published at *OnePeterFive*, *LifeSiteNews*, *The Remnant*, *Catholic Family News*, and *Crisis Magazine*. They have been lightly revised for their inclusion in this volume. To avoid the ungainly sprawl of hyperlinks in the notes, online articles have been referred to simply by author, title, website, and date; when no author is specified, I am the author. Web addresses have been provided for more obscure online locations. Psalms are referenced by their Septuagint/Vulgate numbering. The epigraph from Cardinal Hergenröther is found in the article "Pope" in the old *Catholic Encyclopedia*, vol. 12, pp. 269–70.

March 19, 2022
Feast of St. Joseph
Peter A. Kwasniewski

My Journey from
Ultramontanism to Catholicism

ANY CATHOLICS HAVE HEARD THE word "ultramontanism." But what exactly does it mean? Where did it come from? And why might the phenomenon it describes be harmful—at least today? The Encyclopedia Britannica offers us a handy definition of the term:

> Ultramontanism, from Medieval Latin *ultramontanus*, "beyond the mountains," in Roman Catholicism, a strong emphasis on papal authority and on centralization of the church. The word identified those northern European members of the church who regularly looked southward beyond the Alps (that is, to the popes of Rome) for guidance. During the period of struggle within the church over the extent of papal prerogatives—beginning especially in the 15th century with the conciliar movement and continuing in the following centuries with the growth of strong nationalism and theological liberalism—the Ultramontanists were opposed by those, such as the Gallicans, who wished to restrict papal power. The Ultramontane Party triumphed in 1870 at the first Vatican Council when the dogma of papal infallibility was defined as a matter of Roman Catholic belief.

THE GROWING STRENGTH OF THE PAPACY

We should note, first of all, that the initial desire of Northern Europeans to look towards the papacy in Rome for support and guidance came in the midst of a false theory of conciliarism that attempted to make an ecumenical council—a general synod of bishops—the ultimate authority in the Church, which is clearly contrary to the divine institution of the papal primacy in the Apostle Peter and his successors.

This adherence to the pope gained strength in the period of the Protestant Revolt, for obvious reasons: the Protestants rejected with increasing radicalness the very existence of a single Church of Christ with a single form of government, which led inevitably to doctrinal fragmentation and contradiction. The reforming popes of the Counter-Reformation emerged as the saviors of Christendom, or at least of what portions of it they could salvage in Europe, as well as of the immense additions to the Church that were made through European exploration and conquest.

The spirit of Protestantism gave birth, in the seventeenth and eighteenth centuries, to the rationalism and liberalism of the so-called Enlightenment. In this period, too, the papacy functioned as a visible symbol of continuity with the one Faith of the ancient and medieval Church.

In the revolutionary spirit of the late eighteenth and nineteenth centuries, with the growth of a disordered patriotism and a diseased nationalism, the papacy in Rome, even as it grew progressively weaker in political terms, became just about the only office on earth whose incumbent was, and could be seen to be, transnational and universal, a representative of Christ to the nations and a teacher of all mankind.

Finally, as Protestant liberalism infected the Catholic Church in the nineteenth century and became Modernism, once again the pope showed himself to be a defender of the simplicity, integrity, and totality of the Catholic Faith. This unique role on the world stage made it inevitable that the pope would be understood and seen as the very embodiment of the Catholic Faith, the measure of what it means to be Catholic.

THE POPE AS RALLYING-POINT FOR CATHOLICS

In practical terms, think of what it was like in England or in France in the nineteenth century. England was dominated both by the Established or Anglican Church and by political moderates who were nonetheless basically "liberals" in the Catholic understanding of the term. France was even worse off; her government was dominated by anticlerical Freemasons who continually sought pretexts for opposing the resurgent post-revolutionary Church and who would eventually prevail in their campaign against any kind of union between Church and State. France, moreover, was imbued with centuries-old habits of Jansenism and Gallicanism, which gave rise to a rationalistic and anti-Roman mentality.

In England and in France, the most devout and zealous Catholics tended to exalt the office of the pope, the "Father of Christians," as a counterbalance to regional or national self-interest, a common rallying point for doctrine and discipline. Military imagery has always been favored by Christians, ever since St. Paul's letters and the *Rule* of St. Benedict. The pope could be seen as the general of the Lord's army, mustering troops from the four corners of the earth to engage in battle against the philosophical and political forces of modernity.

In fact, one of the greatest of the nineteenth-century ultra-montanists, a passionate pamphleteer in the cause of Rome and *Romanitas*, was none other than Dom Prosper Guéranger, the beloved author of *The Liturgical Year*, whose book *The Papal Monarchy* in 1870 was one of the most prominent defenses of the doctrine of papal infallibility defined at the First Vatican Council, which adjourned on October 20 of that year (we observed its 150th anniversary in 2020).

THREE DISTINCTIVE MARKS OF THE CATHOLIC

I will come back later on to the actual teaching of the First Vatican Council. For now, I would like to propose that ultramontanism has been the basic mentality of most Catholics in modern times (stretching back several centuries). In the public eye, what makes a man a Catholic is threefold: first, he believes in the Eucharist as the true Body of Christ; second, he venerates the Blessed Virgin Mary; third, he accepts the pope as head of the Church, and follows the pope's teaching. If we take the veneration of Mary as predicated on the privilege of her divine Maternity in the Incarnation, we can see the profound connection between these three (at first sight) disparate truths. In a work published in 1958, at the dusk of Pius XII's pontificate, the great theologian Cardinal Charles Journet beautifully brings out this connection when he says, concerning the bestowal of universal jurisdiction on Peter and his successors:

> What a union of apparently contradictory attributes! What a difficult saying seeking a welcome in our hearts! That Peter, who is one man and who can inhabit only one place, was chosen as head of the Church, which is divine and universal! Nevertheless, in Christianity, this saying is not seen as something strange or foreign to the faith. In a sense, we could say that it sounds to our ears like a familiar and expected message. It formulates a great mystery; but this mystery is in no way new.

In one of its applications, it is the presence of a unique, breathtaking mystery in which Christianity consists: God willed that divine things be enveloped in feebleness, infinite things held fast in space and time. In Luke 1:26-27, at the moment of the Incarnation, we see that all the geographical and genealogical details have been massed together in order to announce to us the descending of Eternity into a moment, Immensity into a place, spiritual Liberty into the constraints of matter. The very Creator of the entire universe was born a small child on our planet and later declares that his flesh is food and his blood drink: these words were spoken in order to unite, but, seeming to many hard and intolerable, they divided. Finally, he proposes a mystery, no doubt inferior but analogous, and he chooses (we could not say his *successor*—this would be blasphemous) his *vicar*, that is, someone to be the authorized spokesman of his teaching and the depositary of a power until now unheard of—a weak man, whose misery Christ knew well and whose denials he publicly foretold.

The Incarnation, the Eucharist, the primacy of Peter, these are the directed manifestations and stages, as it were, of one and the same revelation. There is a worldly wisdom that immediately rejects this revelation. And there is another wisdom that begins to be Christian, begins to believe in the Incarnation, but then, a little farther on, becomes disconcerted before the mystery of the Eucharist or the mystery of the primacy of Peter and makes no further advancement. It seems to forget that God is God, that he passes through matter without being diminished, that, on the contrary, he makes use of matter and transfigures it.[1]

One might put it this way: within the very conception of Christianity, in the mind of its author, the Incarnation was destined to ripple out into the Eucharist, and the Eucharist was to be the sign and cause of the unity of the Church governed by Peter. It is impossible to be Catholic—indeed, impossible to be fully Christian—without believing in the unique visitation of the world by the Son of God made man, without honoring the singular woman

---

1   *The Theology of the Church*, trans. Victor Szczurek, O.Praem. (San Francisco: Ignatius Press, 2004), 128-29.

He chose as His Mother, without accepting His enduring presence among us as our Emmanuel or God-with-us in the Blessed Sacrament, and finally, without remaining subject to His Vicar or representative on earth. There is a tight logic to the fundamental elements of Catholicism: they stand or fall together. Christian reform movements that began by rejecting the papacy ended up, in time, rejecting the Real Presence, the Virgin Birth, and the Incarnation itself. All of these are various forms of one and the same "scandal of the particular": the entrance of God into our material world in order to seek and to save that which was lost.

TEMPTATIONS TO EXAGGERATE THE TRUTH

Given these general truths, which have much to be said for them, it is not surprising that Catholics may develop a "hypertrophic" ultramontanism, a sort of excessive adherence to the person and policies of the pope, by which one simplistically takes everything he says as a definitive judgment and everything he does as a praiseworthy example, wrapping the mantle of infallibility around all his teaching and the garment of impeccability around all his behavior.

Generally, those who operate in this manner are suffering from a double handicap: first, a mighty ignorance of the annals of Church history, which often display the papacy in (shall we say) a less-than-favorable light; and second, a mighty ignorance of the precise understanding of papal infallibility officially taught by the Church.[2]

I decided to call this chapter "My Journey from Ultramontanism to Catholicism" because, as embarrassing as it is to admit it in 2022, my understanding of the papacy during my years in college was papolatrous to an almost satirical degree. I was a "John Paul II" Catholic who believed that the pope had all the right answers

---

2   We also have to take into account the phenomenon that Thomas Pink calls "official theology," which is the "view of the moment" shared by many prelates, theologians, professors, pastors, lay leaders, et al., who do not intend to affirm it solemnly but more or less take it for granted. Every age has its official theology distinct from magisterial teaching; and the former can certainly be in error, as well as occlude the truth by omission. For a full account of this important point, see Thomas Pink, "Vatican II and Crisis in the Theology of Baptism," published in three parts at *The Josias*, November 2, 5, and 8, 2018. It is clear that both exaggerated notions of infallibility and a neglect of traditional qualifications of it have crept in via official theology.

on any and every question, and that the one and only problem we were facing was widespread disobedience to him.

Like many writers, I have kept journals in certain periods of my life, and I'm happy that I possess the one from my senior year at Thomas Aquinas College, in which I stumbled upon this over-the-top passage from April 28, 1994:

> The Pope measures; he is not measured. There is no higher tribunal, no court of appeals; who is to set himself up as judge over the Supreme Pastor, the Vicar of Christ?... He knows more, sees more, hears more, looks towards the future with a higher gauge of utility and worth—charism of his office, grace necessary to fulfill the functions of mother and teacher. No one can be led to *hell* by following his teaching, *per necessitatem*, whereas one risks condemnation for disobeying him, if he speak the words of Christ. Only *per accidens* could his decision lead to damage or distress, as did the words of Christ to Judas: "Go now, be about your business."
>
> A "prudential" decision of the Holy See may or *may not* be right—that is entirely irrelevant to the Catholic. *Religious obedience*: "be silent," "bury the baseball bat," "milk the cows," "let the heretics alone," "permit altar girls," whatever, so long as it does not contradict faith and morals, so long as it pertains to a change in *discipline* and not a change in *dogma*. When the order is promulgated, it is *ipso facto* binding and obligatory, until the Holy See revokes it, or until historical conditions, sufficiently obvious, render it irrelevant... But, if a man have not sufficient wisdom and prudence to decide, he should *always* follow the Pope's decree to the very letter, knowing that the Vicar of Christ can "neither deceive nor be deceived" in his proclamations and orders, when they touch upon *the care of souls*.
>
> The meeting of Christ and the Centurion. What do we learn? "I am a man *accustomed to command*; I say to one man, Go, and he goes..." Christ, marveling, responds: "I have not found *faith* such as this in all of Israel!" Why? Because the Centurion was ready to submit himself to Christ even as his underlings and slaves submit to him, viz. *absolutely*. The Catholic is no milquetoast religionist, he is no Rosary-touting Protestant: he must *obey* the

voice of Peter, or else he forfeits the very thing which separates him from the amorphous Christians who plague the face of the earth.

Not quite a year later, on March 20, 1995, I wrote in a letter to a good friend:

> I maintain ... that the Pope measures, he is not measured. He is "first in the genus," from which all species derive their title, as fire, being the hottest, is the source of heat. The *depositum fidei* does not exist as a separate substance, hovering in the centuries of church history. There is no Magisterium apart from the Pope, who guards and interprets it "like to a householder, who bringeth forth out of his treasury new things and old" (Matthew 13:52). "A good man out of a good treasure bringeth forth good things" (Matthew 12:35). The Pope is the incarnation of the apostolic power and trust, it is he who holds the keys that loose on heaven and on earth. The whole inheritance of the *depositum fidei* rests in his hands, and it is only made living and binding through his mediation. The Pope exercises on earth a role similar to the Virgin Mary in heaven; just as she is the mediatrix of all grace, he is the mediator of all doctrine and discipline. The "constant teaching of the Church" is not simply, or even primarily, historical; it is present, active, animate. Wherein does it reside on earth? In the *Vicarius Christi*; it is like a second nature ingrafted onto him by the working of the Holy Ghost, when he is consecrated Pope.

This, I'm afraid, is a pure and perfect statement of what Italian historian Roberto de Mattei calls "papolatry." As I said, such juvenile exhibitions are frankly embarrassing—but they have the value of demonstrating the absurd overgrowth of a normally healthy instinct, when it is detached from the reality of history and magisterial teaching.

ENTER JOHN HENRY NEWMAN

Earlier I mentioned the growth of ultramontanism in France and England. Not every prominent orthodox Catholic was equally on board with the trend towards papal centralization and exaltation. The man who was arguably the greatest theologian

7

of the nineteenth century, John Henry Newman, was extremely suspicious of the kind of ultramontanism espoused by his fellow countryman William George Ward, who famously and provocatively stated: "I should like a new Papal Bull every morning with my *Times* at breakfast," so that he would have still more beliefs to accept as a Catholic convert. Newman, also of course a Catholic convert from Anglicanism, was distressed at this exaggeration of the papal office and its function. The papacy was at risk of being turned into an industrial factory of new pronouncements and new directives on every subject under the sun.

While Newman's own account of doctrinal development is not immune from criticism, he clearly affirms the immutability of the apostolic deposit of faith and the requirement of complete consistency of any later definition or explanation of a truth with all that has already been held and taught about that truth. In other words, Newman adhered to St. Vincent of Lérins's assumption that if doctrine is to grow or make progress—the word in Latin is *profectus*—it can do so only "according to the same meaning and the same judgment," *in eodem sensu eademque sententia*—a phrase that has been repeated countless times in magisterial documents.[3] Any other kind of change, says St. Vincent, is a corruption, or, in his language, *permutatio*. *Profectus* and *permutatio*: those are the alternatives.

Newman was anxious about such corruption taking place at the First Vatican Council concerning the proposed definition of papal infallibility—a belief on which he thought the less said, the better, not because he did not accept the pope as the God-given pastor of Christians and the final court of appeal, but because he knew that a party of "ultramontanes" was busy pushing a theologically unsound, philosophically unreasonable, historically untenable, and ecclesiastically damaging version of papal inerrancy that threatened to confuse the pope's office with divine revelation itself, rather than seeing him more modestly as the guardian of Tradition and the arbiter of controversy.

"ONE IS OBLIGED TO HOPE..."

Considering the fact that it was none other than Pope Francis who raised Newman to the honors of the altar, the following

3   John Paul II referred to it again in *Veritatis Splendor* (August 6, 1993), n. 53.

excerpt from one of Newman's letters comes across as more than a little ironic. On August 21, 1870, a little over a month after the July 18 promulgation of *Pastor Aeternus*, Newman wrote to his friend Ambrose St. John:

> I have various things to say about the Definition ... [T]o me the serious thing is this, that, whereas it has not been usual to pass definition except in case of urgent and definite necessity, this definition, while it gives the Pope power, creates for him, in the very act of doing so, a precedent and a suggestion to use his power without necessity, when ever he will, when not called on to do so. I am telling people who write to me to have confidence—but I don't know what I shall say to them, if the Pope did so act. And I am afraid moreover, that the tyrant majority [*NB*: this is how Newman refers to the bishops at Vatican I who voted for the definition!] is still aiming at enlarging the *province* of Infallibility. I can only say if all this takes place, we shall in matter of fact be under a new dispensation. But we must hope, for one is obliged to hope it, that the Pope will be driven from Rome, and will not continue the Council, or that there will be another Pope. It is sad he should force us to such wishes.

It is striking to see one of the most brilliant and saintly theologians of modern times entertaining such deep misgivings about an ecumenical Council lawfully convoked, about conciliar acts lawfully promulgated, and especially about the reigning pope, whom he hopes will be driven out of Rome or soon replaced by a better pope. Yet Newman made no attempt to hide where he stood, and although he fully accepted the definition of Vatican I, he also understood it restrictively and modestly, as he argued one should accept all definitions: according to their precise limits and their role within the whole religion of Catholicism.

Those who today have misgivings about the convoking of Vatican II by John XXIII, about various and sundry elements in the sixteen conciliar documents issued under Paul VI, and about the conduct of Pope Francis may take comfort in knowing that such difficulties of mind and problems of conscience are not incompatible with the Catholic Faith or with the virtues of humility and obedience.

9

II

WE HAVE SEEN JOHN HENRY NEWMAN'S REALISTIC and critical assessment of the work of the First Vatican Council, whose dogmas he wholeheartedly accepted but about whose "spirit," if I may so put it, he expressed reservations. Would the definition of papal infallibility prompt popes to start acting like divine oracles, flexing their magisterial muscles at the slightest provocation?

"Bring it on," a blog called *Where Peter Is* would confidently respond. *Where Peter Is* features the work of ardent defenders of Pope Francis and, for that matter, of anything and everything papal. They are, so to speak, those who have never met a papacy they didn't like. If you have run out of creative penances, you may wish to pay the site a visit, but only if you do not suffer from high blood pressure or PTSD (Post-Tridentine Stress Disorder).

Recognizing that Catholicism is inherently a religion of Tradition, *Where Peter Is* sidesteps the awkwardness of patent contradiction between earlier magisterial teaching and Francis's "creativity" by arguing that Tradition actually *means* "whatever the pope says."[4] Tradition is not something given in the past or cumulative, but something constituted by the pope's endorsement of it here and now. Therefore, Catholics *must* assent to *Amoris Laetitia*, the abolition of the death penalty, human fraternity among a plurality of divinely-willed religions,[5] and every other kind of novelty "proposed" by the pope.

THE PAPAL *EX NIHILO*

The heart of the argument is the claim that the pope and bishops are the "interpreters of Tradition" in such a way that we cannot even *know* what Catholic doctrine is unless we are *told* what it is by the pope and bishops. It has no existence *in itself*, apart from their acknowledgment and exposition of it. And if they merely *say* that something *is* Catholic doctrine or is somehow "part of Tradition"—even if it sounds very different from what other popes and bishops used to teach, or even if it's never been said before

---

4   See Mike Lewis, "Followers of the Imagisterium," *Where Peter Is*, January 24, 2019.

5   See John Lamont, "Francis and the Joint Declaration on Human Fraternity: A Public Repudiation of the Catholic Faith," *Rorate Caeli*, February 10, 2019.

by anyone—that's okay, because Tradition is, after all, whatever the current pope and bishops tell us it is (or isn't).

According to this theory, no one could *ever* have a legitimate disagreement with a pope, because such a one would be pitting his own "private interpretation" against the interpreter set up by God.[6] This brand of ultramontanism, like the harangues of my college days quoted earlier, elevates *all* papal statements and policies into authoritative utterances that ought to be trusted on faith as God's will for us today and, accordingly, should never be criticized.

The basic difficulty with this approach is that it makes a hash out of any claim of consistency of teaching on the part of the Catholic Church. If you can get unanimity from the time of the Old and New Testaments to the twenty-first century on the *legitimacy* of capital punishment, but then Pope Francis can declare it contrary to the Gospel and to human dignity (as he very clearly does in his October 11, 2017 address),[7] where are we? Where does that leave us? This line of argument empties Catholicism of any objective content and makes the pope the master rather than the servant of Tradition.[8] Something is wrong if a pope one fine day can make a statement that renders inaccurate or unusable an entire library full of previously approved catechetical, apologetic, theological, and spiritual writings.

How different is the understanding of Pope Benedict XVI, who said in an oft-cited homily in 2005:

> The power that Christ conferred upon Peter and his Successors is, in an absolute sense, a mandate to serve. The power of teaching in the Church involves a commitment to the service of obedience to the Faith. The pope is not an absolute monarch whose thoughts and desires are law. On the contrary: the pope's ministry is a guarantee of obedience to Christ and to his Word. He must not proclaim his own ideas, but rather constantly bind himself

6 See chapter 10.
7 See Address of His Holiness Pope Francis to Participants in the Meeting Promoted by the Pontifical Council for Promoting the New Evangelization, at the Vatican website.
8 See Claudio Pierantoni, "The Need for Consistency between Magisterium and Tradition: Examples from History," in *Defending the Faith Against Present Heresies*, 235–51.

and the Church to obedience to God's Word, in the face of every attempt to adapt it or water it down, and every form of opportunism.... *The pope knows that in his important decisions, he is bound to the great community of faith of all times, to the binding interpretations that have developed throughout the Church's pilgrimage.* Thus, his power is not being above the Word of God, but at the service of it. It is incumbent upon him to ensure that this Word continues to be present in its greatness and to resound in its purity, so that it is not torn to pieces by continuous changes in usage.[9]

This is what well-catechized Catholics had always believed to be the role of the papacy. The pope was expected to make his acts of teaching and governance conform to a Tradition that preexists as a providentially bestowed measure for all believers.

NO NEW DOCTRINES, SAYS VATICAN I

Let us recall the resounding and reassuring words of the First Vatican Council:

> For the Holy Spirit was not promised to the Successors of Peter that they might disclose a new doctrine by His revelation, but rather that, with His assistance, they might reverently guard and faithfully explain the revelation or deposit of faith that was handed down through the Apostles.[10]

The view behind these words furnishes the basis on which the Third Council of Constantinople (680–681)—the sixth of the ecumenical councils—saw itself as competent to issue a crystal-clear condemnation and anathematization of the deceased Pope Honorius (r. 625–638). The conciliar acts were signed by 174 council fathers and the five patriarchal sees, including most importantly that of Rome, where Pope St. Leo II (r. 682–683) endorsed the anathema, repeated it in his own writings, and ordered all the Western bishops to sign off on it.[11]

---

9   Homily for the Mass of Installation as the Bishop of Rome (May 7, 2005), emphasis added.

10   Dogmatic Constitution *Pastor Aeternus* on the Church of Christ (July 18, 1870), Ch. 4, Denzinger-Hünermann 3070.

11   See Roberto De Mattei, *Love for the Papacy and Filial Resistance to the Pope in the History of the Church* (Brooklyn, NY: Angelico Press, 2019), 26.

This view also explains the shadow that hangs over the name of Pope Liberius in the West, as a vacillator who gave encouragement to enemies of the Faith.[12]

The original ultramontanists of the nineteenth century could be forgiven for their enthusiasm. Most of the popes of the Counter-Reformation and post-revolutionary periods in Europe were solidly committed to traditional dogma, liturgy, and morals; the popes from Gregory XVI to Pius X in particular were anti-modern (or anti-Modernist) to the core.[13] They were the heroes fighting the drift into total secularism. We are, regrettably, in a very different place. One who reads Pope St. Pius X's great 1907 encyclical against Modernism, *Pascendi Dominici Gregis,* would find it difficult not to see the opinions he is condemning in the very words of Pope Francis and his supporters.[14]

Note how carefully Benedict XVI, in the quotation above, chooses his every word. He says: "The power of teaching in the Church involves a *commitment* to the service of obedience to the Faith." In other words, it is not involuntary, like the reflex motion of a knee struck with a doctor's rubber mallet. Each bishop, including the bishop of Rome, must make a *voluntary* submission of mind and heart to the Faith, and he can *fail* to do so in the vast realm of statements, decisions, and actions that fall outside the confines of papal infallibility as defined by Vatican I. If a pope's failure to submit himself to Sacred Tradition and to defend it strenuously is notorious enough, it merits condemnation and resistance—a point to which I shall return in a moment.

Pope Benedict continues: "He must not proclaim his own ideas, but rather constantly bind himself and the Church to obedience to God's Word, in the face of every attempt to adapt it or water it down, and every form of opportunism." Implied in this "must" is an *ought*: he ought not to proclaim his own ideas, but choose to bind himself and the Church to what is true, regardless of the pressure of progressive elites.[15] Benedict also insists that the pope should avoid "tearing to pieces the Word of God by continuous

---

12   See Pierantoni, "Need for Consistency."

13   Cf. chapter 9; volume 2, chapters 42 and 49.

14   See volume 2, chapter 62: "Pius X to Francis: From Modernism Expelled to Modernism Enthroned."

15   See volume 2, chapter 33.

changes in usage." It seems that Paul VI never received that memo. In almost every area of the Church's life, he attempted to change what his predecessors—including the popes immediately before him—had established.[16] Francis, like Paul VI, has attempted, directly and indirectly, to overturn the magisterium of *his* predecessors as well. One can see this in his approach to *Veritatis Splendor* on moral absolutes, *Familiaris Consortio* on the indissolubility of marriage, *Humanae Vitae* on contraception, and much else besides.[17]

EVEN BAD BISHOPS REMAIN BISHOPS

In the fourth century, during the Arian crisis that swept through the Church, most of the bishops stopped defending Catholic Tradition. To put it bluntly, they were either heretics or cowards. St. Athanasius of Alexandria, St. Hilary of Poitiers, and just a few others whom we now revere as confessors of the Faith claimed that their brother bishops—in the *hundreds*—were renegades.

Did this mean that all of those bishops ceased to be successors of the Apostles? No. Did they lose their authority to govern? No. They remained what they were divinely ordained to be. But they were not living up to the demands of their office; they were not living by the charism of truth entrusted to them. By the *sensus fidei* or divine instinct for the truth, the faithful were able to detect the difference between the Arians and the Catholics; they purposefully avoided the former and sought out the latter. St. Athanasius was faithful to the office that Christ gave him, but he was hounded out of his see multiple times by his opponents and died from maltreatment at the hands of Arians and Semi-Arians who had the backing of "successors of the Apostles." The laity supported Athanasius because they recognized in his doctrine the truth of the Faith proclaimed immutably at Nicaea.

Having an apostolic office makes a bishop worthy of honor and obedience—but he still has to work out his own salvation "in fear and trembling" (Phil. 2:12), like everyone else. He still has to profess the Faith by an act of free will supported by God's grace. He still has to submit to the same Tradition to which every other Catholic from the day of Pentecost to the Second Coming has to

---

16   See "The New Synthesis of All Heresies: On Nietzschean Catholicism," *OnePeterFive*, May 16, 2018.

17   See volume 2, chapter 15.

submit.[18] And, if I may be allowed to lapse into slang, he can blow it big time, just like the rest of us. As it says in Scripture, the mighty, if they fail, "shall be mightily tormented" (Wis. 6:6). It's not for nothing that Dante puts popes and bishops in his *Inferno*.

CAN WE CONDEMN OR RESIST A POPE?

A moment ago I spoke of condemnation and resistance. I want to clarify this point because it is very important.

"Condemnation" of papal error coming from a layman or a simple priest or even a diocesan bishop could not be a definitive judgment, such as that which the Third Council of Constantinople passed posthumously on Honorius. It could only ever be a respectful expression of one's conscientious conviction that a pope had gone astray, based on objective criteria.

All the more impossible would it be for laymen or clergy to conclude that a pope had ceased to be pope, or that he had never become pope in the first place.[19] Whoever reigns as pope, acknowledged to be such by the unanimity or generality of cardinals, bishops, and faithful, must be endured, for good or for ill. Although it is theoretically possible that an imperfect council consisting of

18   See "Why Catholicism is necessarily dogmatic, with a definite content," *LifeSiteNews*, February 12, 2019.

19   The sedevacantists quote reams of authorities to the effect that heretics are severed from the Body of the Church, and therefore, they conclude, may not hold or continue to hold ecclesiastical office. This line of reasoning is too simplistic. No private individual or lay Catholic has the authority to declare, in a manner that would be binding on himself and others, that a certain bishop or pope is or must be considered deposed due to apostasy, heresy, or schism. We can recognize heresy, call it out, refuse to adopt it, and warn others to be wary of it, but ultimately it has to be a bishop (such as a metropolitan archbishop) who corrects and deposes a bishop, and an imperfect council that confronts and admonishes a heretic pope and declares him deposed by God should the heresy be unrenounced (though Bishop Athanasius Schneider has argued that not even this recourse is possible, and that we must suffer while resisting: see his "On the Question of a Heretical Pope," *OnePeterFive*, March 20, 2019). If a pope is a heretic, *we* know what *we* must do; that is all we can do. His status is for the college of cardinals or the episcopacy to adjudicate. Nor is this a matter of "punting" on the question; it's a matter of honoring the apostolic hierarchical constitution of the Church. Whether our bishops are doing a splendid job or a deplorable job, it's still *their* job to do it. At this juncture they are making an absolute mess of it, admittedly, but that's on their head, and we must pray for them to get some courage and wisdom.

either cardinals or bishops could declare that a pope, due to his contumacious adherence to heresy or his apostasy, has been *ipso facto* deposed by God, I have not met a single person who actually believes that our cardinals or bishops today, or even a representative number thereof, will ever come together for this purpose, so the question, however fascinating it may be, is moot.

Some neo-ultramontanists contest whether any Catholic of any degree may condemn or resist a pope in his teaching or prudential decisions. The more "street-smart" approach of our forefathers to this question may be seen in quotations from eminent and approved Catholic theologians.

Speaking of fraternal correction in the *Summa*, St. Thomas Aquinas famously says: "If the Faith were endangered, a subject ought to rebuke his prelate even publicly."[20] A century later, Juan Cardinal de Torquemada (1388–1468) states: "Were the pope to command anything against Holy Scripture, or the articles of faith, or the truth of the Sacraments, or the commands of the natural or divine law, he ought not to be obeyed, but in such commands is to be ignored."[21]

RESIST TO HIS FACE

The Renaissance Thomist Cardinal Cajetan (1469–1534), born one year after Torquemada's death, counsels: "You must resist, to his face, a pope who is openly tearing the Church apart—for example, by refusing to confer ecclesiastical benefices except for money, or in exchange for services... A case of simony, even committed by a pope, must be denounced."[22] Cajetan is talking about simony, which was obviously a massive problem in centuries past; but it is far from being the worst sin or the greatest problem. The imposition of harmful discipline such as the promulgation of a valid but inadequate and inauthentic liturgy, or an assault on the integrity of doctrine, is certainly worse than simony.

One of the greatest Jesuit theologians, Francisco Suárez (1548–1617), declares: "If the Pope lays down an order contrary to right customs one does not have to obey him; if he tries to do something

---

20   *Summa theologiae* II-II, qu. 33, art. 4, ad 2. See Paul Casey, "Can a Catholic Ever Disobey a Pope?," *OnePeterFive*, July 17, 2020.

21   De Torquemada, *Summ. de Eccl.*, pp. 47–48.

22   Cajetan, *De Comparatione Auctoritatis Papae et Concilii.*

manifestly opposed to justice and to the common good, it would be licit to resist him; if he attacks by force, he could be repelled by force, with the moderation characteristic of a good defense."[23]

Sylvester Prieras (1456–1523), "a Dominican theologian, appointed master of the Sacred Palace by Pope Leo X and known for his detailed rebuttal to Luther's 95 Theses,"[24] has these surprisingly vigorous words to say:

> In answer to the question, "What should be done in cases where the Pope destroys the Church by his evil actions?" [I reply]: "He would certainly sin; he should neither be permitted to act in such fashion, nor should he be obeyed in what was evil; but he should be resisted with a courteous reprehension.... He does not have the power to destroy; therefore, if there is evidence that he is doing it, it is licit to resist him. The result of all this is that if the Pope destroys the Church by his orders and acts, he can be resisted and the execution of his mandate prevented. The right of open resistance to prelates' abuse of authority stems also from natural law.[25]

Similarly, St. Robert Bellarmine (1542–1621), Doctor of the Church and preeminent theologian of the Counter-Reformation, wrote:

> As it is lawful to resist the pope, if he assaulted a man's person, so it is lawful to resist him, if he assaulted souls, or troubled the state, and much more if he strove to destroy the Church. It is lawful, I say, to resist him, by not doing what he commands, and hindering the execution of his will; still, it is not lawful to judge or punish or even depose him, because he is nothing other than a superior.[26]

In that last phrase, Bellarmine is strictly correct: no one on earth could depose a pope, since it is only an inferior who can

---

23   Suárez, *De Fide*, disp. X, sect. VI, n. 16; *De Fide*, disp. X, sec VI, no. 16.
24   The description is from Casey, "Can a Catholic Ever Disobey a Pope?"
25   Prieras, *Dialogus de Potestate Papae* (from Francisco de Vitoria: *Obras*, pp. 486–87). Francisco de Vitoria (1483–1546) himself says: "If the Pope by his orders and his acts destroys the Church, one can resist him and impede the execution of his commands."
26   Bellarmine, *De Romano Pontifice*, Bk. 2, ch. 29, seventh reply.

be deposed by his superior. However, as we said earlier, it is possible that an imperfect council of cardinals and/or bishops could declare a pope who is known to be formally heretical of having been deposed by Almighty God—for surely, no one believes that God is not the pope's superior.

THE NEED FOR STUDY

Have there been instances in Church history where condemnation has been called for and resistance has been exercised? Absolutely: dozens of times. The most readable, interesting, and important book on the subject is Roberto de Mattei's *Love for the Papacy and Filial Resistance to the Pope in the History of the Church* (Angelico, 2019). I cannot recommend this book too highly. I would also recommend Henry Sire's *Phoenix from the Ashes: The Making, Unmaking and Restoration of Catholic Tradition* (Angelico, 2015).

Sometimes traditional Catholics are presented with the objection: "Should we all have to be theologians and historians to maneuver our way in the Church today? Surely, that's not what Jesus had in mind. He wanted simple faith and trust." This objection is true in one way and false in another. It is true in the sense that the Catholic Faith is indeed accessible to all and at all times: what we need to know and to do in order to be saved is mercifully compact. We find it in the Creeds and Commandments taught by the Church in all of her trustworthy old catechisms. In this sense, one who knows his catechism knows what the truth is and how to get to Heaven.

We are, however, in a period unique in history. Never before have the basic tenets of the Creed, the elementary Commandments of God, and the traditional divine worship of the Church been so assaulted, ripped apart, and undermined as they are in modern times, particularly with the resurgence of Modernism right before, during, and after the Second Vatican Council. What Catholics in former ages had the luxury of taking for granted, what every bishop and pastor taught from the pulpit, what every catechism given the *imprimatur* would have contained, can no longer be assumed to be what we will find when we walk into a church, pick up a document, or buy the latest catechism. For this reason, it is incumbent on us, more than it would ordinarily be for laity in a healthy period of time, to study our Faith, to understand at least the rudiments of the revolution that has occurred, and to hold fast to the Catholicism that the saints lived and handed on—with simple faith and trust.

Catholics who protest the novelties of Francis are not setting up their "private judgment" against "God's judgment." Rather, such Catholics are looking at the witness of twenty centuries, twenty-one councils, and two-hundred-sixty-five popes preceding this one and seeing contradictions on any number of points, using our God-given gift of reason, which can indeed tell us infallibly that—contrary to papal cheerleader Fr. Antonio Spadaro, S. J.—two plus two equals *four* and *cannot* equal five.

III

IN THE FIRST PART, I DEFINED ULTRAMONTANISM, explained why it arose, and analyzed the danger of it when taken as an attitude that makes more of the papacy than it was intended to be, or rather, makes it *other* than it was intended to be. In the second part, I looked at an extreme current example of this hyperpapalism, namely, the blog *Where Peter Is*, and quoted theologians on why and when Catholics are authorized to condemn or resist a pope.

"What good, then, is having a pope?" someone might be tempted to ask. "On your account, we'd be better off without one."

My response is that (1) this is certainly not true, if we look at the many saintly and valiant popes who have defended and, when necessary, defined the Deposit of Faith down through the centuries, and (2) a pope benefits the Church when, and precisely inasmuch as, he exercises his office well.

Frustration with the papacy occurs only for those who have an exaggerated notion of the pope's role. For the most part, Catholics throughout history have been able to ignore what the pope was doing, because they already knew their faith—what they had to believe, pray for, do, and shun. For its part, Vatican I is clear about the specific circumstances within which the Church's infallibility is engaged by her earthly head.[27] The pope is supposed to be "where the buck stops" when there is a dispute that cannot be otherwise resolved. He is meant to be, as Cardinal Newman says, a *remora* or barrier against doctrinal innovation, not an engine for

---

27 See Fr. Fortescue's summary below, pp. 29–30.

doctrinal development, let alone a chatterbox sharing his personal opinions in newspaper interviews or airborne press conferences.[28] A priest writing under the pen name Pauper Peregrinus observes:

> Was it also from being thus weakened in their sense of their own prerogatives that orthodox bishops came to depend too much on Rome to teach the unpopular doctrines, for example on sexual morality? While we were blessed with many fine papal encyclicals in the 19th and 20th centuries, it is not a healthy sign when letters from the Roman Pontiff to the universal Church become the usual means by which orthodoxy is maintained among Catholics. The episcopacy is the normal means for doing this; the papacy exists to scotch errors that episcopal teaching has not been able to defeat. Whether the massive increase, in modern times, of papal documents directed to the universal Church is related as cause or as effect of a dearth of good episcopal teaching is a nice question.[29]

In fact, the gravity of the papal office is such, and so great the responsibility, that a pope should be characterized by saying rather *less* than most bishops or priests do, instead of saying more. He should be a man of few and serious words, a "prisoner of the Vatican" (so to speak) who, instead of globetrotting, works tirelessly to put the Church's house in order by a rigorous selection of orthodox bishops and the appointment of collaborators exceptional for orthodoxy, holiness, and zeal for souls. Is this too much to ask? If we look at what St. Pius V and St. Pius X did, we can see that it is certainly not too much to expect.

HOW THE POPE IS LIKE ST. JOSEPH

I find it helpful to reflect on how the pope plays a role not unlike that of St. Joseph towards the Virgin and Child. Christ, the Word, has His origin from elsewhere; Joseph is not His natural father, but only His protector. The Virgin, image of the Church, is more exalted than her husband, but nevertheless under his care and authority. Joseph is "the Just Man" because he never

---

28   See Fr. John Hunwicke, "Peter Says No," *First Things*, February 7, 2017.
29   "Papal Infallibility After One Hundred and Fifty Years," *OnePeterFive*, July 20, 2020.

exceeds or falls short of the role he has been given, which places him at once in subordination to his wife and foster Child, and in a certain position of governance over them. But St. Joseph is also "the Silent Man": not a single word of his is recorded in Scripture. He does what he is asked to do, without making a scene, without excess verbiage, and without the need to shine. No wonder there was barely any cult of St. Joseph for the first 1,500 years of Christianity. He hid himself in the shadows. Looking at the popes across history, we might ask ourselves which ones have acted the most like St. Joseph, and which ones the least.

John Henry Newman helps us to grasp the Catholic religion as something whole, complex, sublime, and coherent, in which we do not see the papacy looming as a dominating protuberance out of all proportion with the rest of the body, but as one piece in a brightly-colored mosaic designed by the divine Craftsman. Newman gratefully acknowledges the pope's crucial role but refuses to make of him the originator or measure of Christian doctrine or Christian life. This is why I believe Newman would have had just the same reaction to Cardinal Müller's "Manifesto of Faith"[30] as Fr. John Hunwicke did (another convert from Anglicanism):

> Silence can say more than a million words. Conan Doyle's dog, for example, that did *not* bark in the night. I think the most striking thing about the Manifesto given us by Gerhard Cardinal Mueller was what it did *not* mention . . . the Papacy.
>
> Just consider the amount of controversy the question of the Petrine Ministry created at the time of Vatican I; how much controversy there has been between Catholic and non-Catholic polemicists. Consider the Personality Cult which has surrounded popes since, I think, roughly the last part of the pontificate of Blessed Pius IX. A cult that treats the Roman Bishop like a demi-god or a pop star . . . . I think it is sentimental and mawkish, sickly, corrupt and corrupting. It was certainly not invented by PF and his cronies, but it has reached a new *theological* peak in this pontificate. Curial cronies tell us that the Holy Spirit speaks through PF's mouth; the English bishops write letters to inform him that

---

30   For the full text in English, see "Cardinal Müller issues Manifesto: A quasi correction of Pope Francis' pontificate," *LifeSiteNews*, February 8, 2019.

the Holy Spirit was responsible for his election and guides him daily; a [certain] Fr Rosica, incredibly, explains to us that the pope is free from the encumbrances of Scripture and Tradition. It is what I have called 'Bergoglianism'. I think it is not only sick in itself, but is a dangerous poison of rare toxicity within the Church Militant.

Yet, despite all this, Cardinal Mueller did not even mention this enormous elephant in a tiny room, even in passing. I have not felt so refreshed for a long time.[31]

Of course, the refreshment soon passes as we realize once again, with a groan, that we *are* living in a world and in a Church in which Newman's wise reservations about the role of the pope and Cardinal Müller's confidence in basic Catholic doctrine are not shared by a large number of the bishops, especially the Bishop of Rome at their head—in spite of the fact that, precisely as successors of the Apostles, they are solemnly committed to their Joseph-like role of guarding the holiness of our Mother and providing a home worthy to be dwelt in by Christ.

WHY PETER IS THE ROCK

Peter—the original Peter and each of his successors—is called a "rock" *by holding and publicly professing the immovable truth of Christ and His Church*. This is not a subjective faith to be determined by each generation, or customized by each new pope, but rather the common faith of the Church, which each of us receives as a member of the Mystical Body of Christ. This is the faith that waxes strong in any Christian who has learned his catechism well and who knows, by a supernatural instinct, what is true and compatible with the truth, and what is heretical or offensive to pious ears. If the Faith was supposed to be changeable and changing, Christ would have named Peter "water" or "mud," not "rock."

In a time of confusion, one thing is clear: we must hold fast to the settled and articulate Tradition of the Church: in her doctrine (e.g., what we find thoroughly spelled out in a careful compilation like Ludwig Ott's *Fundamentals of Catholic Dogma*); in our moral life, according to the constant teaching and example of the saints; above all, in her liturgical worship, her authentic

---

31 "Without the Father...Cardinal Mueller's Manifesto (1)," *Fr Hunwick's Mutual Enrichment*, February 15, 2019.

age-old rites. This is what we are asked to do: *remain faithful* to the inheritance we have received, prior to the period of anarchy.

To the objector who says: "this traditionalist position is subjective!," I reply: No, it is not. The Catholic Tradition includes generally accepted readings of Scripture by the Church Fathers and Doctors as well as copious magisterial determinations, such as the dogmas and anathemas of ecumenical Councils. There are numerous objective and mutually reinforcing indications of Catholic teaching, and these constitute true *limits* on what the current Magisterium (pope/bishops) may legitimately teach, or what a Catholic today may accept as rationally consistent. If you are put in a situation where you must, in effect, deny both your faith in the past guidance of the Church by the Holy Spirit *and* your reason—which tells you, according to available evidence and sound argumentation, that one thing is better or worse than another—in order to cling to a self-destructive path chosen by Church officials, how are you different from a Calvinist who denies that faith and reason have anything to do with one another, or a Mormon who has neither faith nor reason to bank on? "A priorism" is all well and good, but it is a short step from that to the most blind and pathetic fideism that has ever been seen.

The conservative, by indiscriminately taking "the Magisterium of the Moment" as his guide in all things, unmoors himself from the established content of cumulative teaching and risks being guided by the whims of a capricious monarch or the synthetic dogmas of an ideologue. The conservative would have no basis for questioning or disagreeing with anything a pope emits, no matter how much it departed from the teaching of his predecessors or even that of Scripture. Such a view effectively infallibilizes in one fell swoop the current Magisterium or the current pope of Rome, thereby dissenting from Vatican I's understanding of the infallibility that Christ willed *the Church* to possess.[32]

"BACCI BALL"

In the first part of this chapter, I quoted some passages from journals written in my college years, when, intoxicated with John Paul II's stardom, I espoused an extreme ultramontanism as the solution to all evils. In the second part, I noted that today an entire

---

32   See Pauper Peregrinus, "Papal Infallibility"; cf. chapter 13.

website caters to this death-defying sport. We find a rather startling exhibit in the otherwise edifying book *Meditations for Each Day* written by Cardinal Antonio Bacci, the Vatican's chief Latinist under four successive popes (Pius XI, Pius XII, John XXIII, and Paul VI):

> There is in the world... one man in whom the greatness of God is reflected in the most outstanding way of all. He participates in the authority and in a certain sense in the personality of Christ. This man is the Vicar of Jesus Christ, the Pope.... His power extends to the ends of the world and is under the protection of God, Who has promised to confirm in Heaven whatever he will decree upon earth. His dignity and authority, then, are almost divine. Let us bow humbly before such greatness. Let us promise to obey the Pope as we would Christ.... We cannot dispute or murmur against anything which he teaches or decrees. To disobey the Pope is to disobey God. To argue or murmur against the Pope is to argue or murmur against Jesus Himself. When we are confronted with His commands, we have only one choice—absolute obedience and complete surrender.[33]

A sport that involves this level of danger might well be called, tongue-in-cheek, "Bacci ball." The good cardinal himself, however, had to give up on it. The years 1967 and 1969 saw Bacci stand forth, almost alone in the college of cardinals, in acts of noble and courteous opposition to the line being taken by Pope Paul VI. As befitted a man of letters and a passionate lover of Latin, these acts took the form of critiques of the liturgical reform.

The first was Bacci's own preface to Tito Casini's diatribe against the vulgarization of the liturgy, *The Torn Tunic*, in which he made no attempt to hide his disapproval of the unceremonious murder of the Latin-rite Church's mother tongue. The second was Bacci's willingness to add his name to the cover letter of *The Short Critical Study of the New Order of Mass* written by a group of Roman

---

33 *Meditations for Each Day* (Waterloo, ON: Arouca Press, 2018), 26–28. This work was originally published in Italian in 1959, at the end of Pius XII's reign. Its English translation appeared in 1965, the year when Paul VI offered the first-ever Italian Mass at the Ognissanti in Rome. See "Dom Alcuin Reid on the 50th Anniversary of Mass in the Vernacular," *New Liturgical Movement*, March 7, 2015.

theologians. Although many high-ranking prelates had initially agreed to sign it (Archbishop Marcel Lefebvre claimed that six hundred prelates would have done so), everyone got proverbial cold feet when the text was prematurely leaked. In the end, it was sent to Paul VI with only two signatures: Cardinal Ottaviani's—and Cardinal Bacci's.

This act of courage will be remembered for centuries to come, no less than Paul VI's villainy in allowing the magnificent liturgy of the Church of Rome to be defiled.[34]

THIS TRIAL IS FOR TESTING AND PURIFYING US

It is true that at a tense moment like this, we can become impatient and frustrated at the inaction of our episcopal shepherds, who ought *at very least* to be condemning rampant errors and evil actions (e.g., the Buenos Aires guidelines, the death penalty error, the Pachamama veneration, the Abu Dhabi statement, etc.). It is at just such times that we are proved like gold in the furnace, our patience is put to the test, and we grow in our trust in Divine Providence and our fervor in crying out to Him for intervention.

The worst thing we could do is to abandon ship for one or another branch of the Eastern Orthodox, or for the imaginary green pastures of sedevacantism, on the pretext that somehow these groups are "better off" than we are. What good would this move accomplish? It would only *remove* good people from where they are most needed—*within* the visible hierarchical Body of Christ—and would only contribute further to the scandal of Christians divided amongst themselves. What is needed is steadfast attachment to the Bride of Christ, in spite of her marred countenance on earth; unswerving loyalty to her eternal Head; and total acceptance of the doctrine He entrusted to her in its integrity.

We are living through an unprecedented time. So many "certainties" have been blown up as by grenades and bombs. The one and only safe path is to stick to what we know to be *certain*; to implore God's help and intervention daily; to entrust oneself to the Virgin Mary; and not to venture into dangerous trackless territory, such as holding that the one accepted as pope is not the

---

34   On the history of the *Short Critical Study* otherwise known as *The Ottaviani Intervention*, see the preface to the edition prepared by the late Rev. Anthony Cekada (West Chester, OH: Philothea Press, 2010).

pope,[35] or that the new Mass is invalid, etc. These conclusions are by no means *necessitated* by the problems, but they are tempting as pressure-release valves that make us feel like we are "doing something" against the evil, "rejecting" it, when all the while we are giving into subtler evils.[36] In fact, it is precisely the validity of this renegade papacy and the sacramental validity of this fabricated Mass that make our lot so much worse, and the duty of fidelity and reparation so much more urgent.[37]

DON'T GET A CRICK IN THE NECK

We are duty-bound to pray for our shepherds—and then, with a cheerful countenance and a jaunty step, get on with our daily lives as Catholics. For most of her history, the Church has bustled along in her mission, without waiting to hear the latest address by the pope or counting the bishops' votes at the latest synod. What we need to believe and to do has been laid out for us for a long time, with no possibility that it will ever be substantially changed. For this reason, we don't need to get a crick in the neck by always looking over our shoulder towards Rome, wondering what's the latest revelation (good or evil) from the Casa Santa Marta.

The city of Rome houses the bones of at least a hundred popes, most of whom are forgotten by all but historians. Visitors to St. Peter's basilica walk past one sarcophagus after another as they proceed toward the *confessio* to pay homage to the Prince of the Apostles. Soon, the wretched papacy under which we now suffer will be past, as we draw closer, step by step, to the final confrontation of Christ with Antichrist. Let the dead bury the dead; let modernists bury modernists. "As for you," says the Lord to each of us, "follow Me."

I realize the foregoing advice does not clear up our difficulties, which remain stubbornly opaque and undeniably menacing. For

---

35   See Eric Sammons, "Is Francis the Pope?," *OnePeterFive*, October 29, 2019.
36   See Michael Massey, "Sedevacantism Is Modern Luciferianism," *OnePeterFive*, December 2, 2019. Here, "Luciferianism" refers to the movement started by Bishop Lucifer of Cagliari (d. 370/71) at the time of the Arian crisis.
37   See Bishop Athanasius Schneider, "Sins Against the Blessed Sacrament and the Need of a Crusade of Eucharistic Reparation," in Peter Kwasniewski, *The Holy Bread of Eternal Life: Restoring Eucharistic Reverence in an Age of Impiety* (Manchester, NH: Sophia Institute Press, 2020), 273-85. Also available online.

basic sanity, it is crucial at this time to recognize that we *are* in uncharted waters, in the midst of a tempest like none other. There will be no "easy solutions"; those proffered by hyperpapalists and antipapalists are no better than the simplifications (*sola fide, sola gratia, sola Scriptura*) by which Protestantism thought to escape from the corruption of the late medieval Church and purchased instead centuries of fissiparous woe. This is surely a mess that only an omniscient and omnipotent God could sort out, a mess from which only He could deliver us, in answer to the prayers He would call forth from our weary but undefeated souls.

That is why I repeat: our sanctifying work, planned for us by God in His eternal Providence, is to remain faithful to tradition and to prayer, come what may; to bide our time, keep our sanity, hold steady, and wait for the Lord. He is not far away in utopian pastures; He is still and always among us. "Behold, I am with you all days, even to the consummation of the world" (Mt. 28:20).

2

Lessons from Church History:
A Brief Review of
Papal Lapses

T HERE ARE THOSE IN THE CHURCH WHO
cannot bear to see a pope criticized for any reason—as if
the whole Catholic Faith would come tumbling down were
we to show that a particular successor of Peter was a scoundrel,
murderer, fornicator, coward, compromiser, ambiguator, espouser
of heresy, or promoter of faulty discipline. But it is quite false that
the Faith would come tumbling down; it is far stronger, stabler,
and sounder than that, because it does not *depend* on any particular
incumbent of the papal office. Rather, it precedes these incumbents;
outlasts them; and, in fact, judges them as to whether they have
been good or bad vicars of Christ. The Faith is entrusted to the
popes, as it is to the bishops, but it is not subject to their control.

The Catholic Faith comes to us from God, from Our Lord Jesus
Christ, who is the Head of the Church, its immovable cornerstone,
its permanent guarantee of truth and holiness.[1] The content of
that Faith is *not* determined by the pope. It is determined by Christ
and handed down in Sacred Scripture, Sacred Tradition, and the
Magisterium—with the Magisterium understood not as anything
and everything that emanates from bishops or popes, but as the
cumulative public, official, definitive, and universal teaching of the
Church enshrined in dogmatic canons and decrees, anathemas,
bulls, encyclicals, and other instruments of teaching in harmony
with the foregoing.

One serious problem that faces us is a "papalism" that blinds
Catholics to the reality that popes are peccable and fallible human
beings like the rest of us, and that their pronouncements are

---

1   On the changelessness of the Faith that derives from Christ's nature
and mission, see chapter 7 below; cf. "The Cult of Change and Christian
Changelessness" in Peter Kwasniewski, *Ministers of Christ: Recovering the Roles
of Clergy and Laity in an Age of Confusion* (Manchester, NH: Crisis Publications,
2021), 235–46.

guaranteed to be free from error only under strictly delimited conditions.[2] Fr. Adrian Fortescue formulates it thus:

> *Providence will see to it that the Pope shall never commit the Church to error in a matter of religion.* This is the famous "infallibility" of the First Vatican Council. It is as well to state again plainly what it does mean. It does not mean any sort of inspiration given to the Pope. It does not mean that he will always know or understand more about our religion than anyone else. A Pope might be quite ignorant and a very poor theologian. He may make a mistake as a private theologian; only God will take care that he does not commit the whole Church to it. Papal infallibility is a negative protection. We are certain that God will not allow a certain thing to happen; that is all. It does not mean that the Pope will always give the wisest or best decision or that what he says will always be well advised or opportune. He may not speak at all; he may preserve a regrettable silence, just when it would be greatly to the good of the Church if he did speak. But if he does speak, and if he speaks in such a way as to commit the Church, then what he says will not be false. It maybe inadequate.
>
> When does the Pope so speak as to commit the whole Church? This is what we mean by a decision *ex cathedra.* The First Vatican Council defined that the Pope's decisions *ex cathedra* cannot be false. It says nothing about

---

2   For a luminous exposition, see the article called "Infallibility" at Fish-eaters (www.fisheaters.com/papolatry.html). I define "papalism" or its more extreme version "papolatry" as follows. If the Faith is seen more as "what the reigning pope is saying" (simply speaking) than "what the Church has always taught" (taken collectively), we are dealing with a false exaltation of the person and office of the pope. As Ratzinger said many times, the pope is the servant of Tradition, not its master; he is bound by it, not in power over it. Of course, the pope can and will make doctrinal and disciplinary determinations, but relatively few things he says are going to make the cut for formal infallibility. All that he teaches *qua* pope (when he appears to be *intending* to teach in that manner) should be received with respect and submission, unless there is something in it that is simply contrary to what has been handed down before. If, e.g., a synod on marriage and family or its papal byproduct attempts to force on the Church a teaching or a discipline contrary to the Faith, we cannot accept it and must resist.

any other kind of papal pronouncement; it explains an "*ex cathedra*" statement as (1) a definition, (2) of dogma on faith or morals, (3) binding on the whole Church. This leaves the Pope as much power of expressing his opinion on any subject as anyone else, of expressing it as forcibly as he thinks necessary, yet without committing us to any theory of special divine protection for such statements, unless he satisfies these conditions.[3]

Apart from that, the realm of papal ignorance, error, sin, and disastrous prudential governance is broad and deep—although secular history affords no catalog of greatness comparable to the nearly 100 papal saints,[4] and plenty of worse examples than the worst popes, which says a lot about man's fallen condition.

At a time when Catholics are confused about whether and how a pope can go wrong, it seems useful to compile examples in three categories: (1) times when the popes were guilty of grave personal immorality; (2) times when popes connived at or with heresy, or were guilty of a harmful silence or ambiguity in regard to heresy; (3) times when popes taught (albeit not *ex cathedra*) something heretical, savoring of heresy, or harmful to the faithful.

Not everyone may agree that every item listed is, in fact, a full-blooded example of the category in question, but that is beside the point; the fact that there are a *number* of problematic instances is sufficient to show that popes are not automatic oracles of God who hand down only what is good, right, holy, and laudable. If that last statement seems like a caricature, one need only look at how conservative Catholics today are bending over backward to get lemonade out of every lemon offered by Pope Francis and denying with vehemence that Roman lemons could ever be rotten or poisonous.

POPES GUILTY OF GRAVE PERSONAL IMMORALITY

This, sadly, is an easy category to fill, and it need not detain us much. One might take as examples six figures about whom Chamberlin wrote.[5]

---

3   *The Early Papacy* (San Francisco, Ignatius Press, 2008), 47–48.
4   See the next chapter.
5   E. R. Chamberlin, *The Bad Popes* (Dorchester: Dorset Press, 1994).

JOHN XII (955–964) gave land to a mistress, murdered several people, and, so the sources say, was killed by a man who caught him in bed with the man's wife.

BENEDICT IX (1032–1044, 1045, 1047–1048) managed to be pope three times, having sold the office off and bought it back again.

URBAN VI (1378–1389) complained that he did not hear enough screaming when cardinals who had conspired against him were tortured.

ALEXANDER VI (1492–1503) bribed his way to the throne and bent all of his efforts to the advancement of his illegitimate children, such as Lucrezia, whom at one point he made regent of the papal states, and Cesare, admired by Machiavelli for his bloody ruthlessness. In his reign, debauchery reached an unequaled nadir: for a certain banquet, Alexander VI brought in fifty Roman prostitutes to engage in a public orgy for the viewing pleasure of the invited guests. Such was the scandal of his pontificate that his clergy refused to bury him in St. Peter's after his death.

LEO X (1513–1521) was a profligate Medici who once spent a seventh of his predecessors' reserves on a single ceremony. To his credit, he published the papal bull *Exsurge Domine* (1520) against the errors of Martin Luther, within which he condemned, among others, the proposition: "That heretics be burned is against the will of the Spirit" (n. 33).

CLEMENT VII (1523–1534), also a Medici, by his power-politicking with France, Spain, and Germany, managed to get Rome sacked.

There are others one could mention.

STEPHEN VII (896–897) hated his predecessor, Pope Formosus, so much that he had him exhumed, tried, de-fingered, and thrown in the Tiber, while (falsely) declaring ordinations given at his hands to have been invalid. Had this ill-advised declaration stood, it would have affected the spiritual lives of many, since the priests would not have been confecting the Eucharist or absolving sins.

PIUS II (1458–1464) penned an erotic novel before he became pope.

INNOCENT VIII (1484–1492) was the first pope to acknowledge officially his bastards, loading them with favors.

PAUL III (1534–1549), who owed his cardinalate to his sister, the mistress of Alexander VI, and himself the father of bastards, made two grandsons cardinals at the ages of fourteen and sixteen and waged war to obtain the Duchy of Parma for his offspring.

URBAN VIII (1623–1644) engaged in abundant nepotism and supported the castration of boys so they could sing in his papal choir as *castrati*. Cardinals denounced him, with Cardinal Ludovisi actually threatening to depose him as a protector of heresy.

There are debates about the extent of the wrongdoing of some of these popes, but even with all allowances made, we must admit, with a sigh, that a papal hall of shame exists.

POPES WHO CONNIVED AT HERESY OR WERE GUILTY OF HARMFUL SILENCE OR AMBIGUITY

POPE ST. PETER (d. ca. 64). It may seem daring to begin with St. Peter, but after all, he did shamefully compromise on the application of an article of faith, viz., the equality of Jewish and Gentile Christians and the abolition of the Jewish ceremonial law—a lapse for which he was rebuked to his face by St. Paul (cf. Gal. 2:11). This has been commented on so extensively by the Fathers and Doctors of the Church and by more recent authors that it needs no special treatment here. It should be pointed out that Our Lord, in His Providence, allowed His first vicar to fail more than once so that we would not be scandalized when it happened again with his successors. This, too, is why He chose Judas: so the treason of bishops would not cause us to lose faith that He remains in command of the Church and of human history.

POPE LIBERIUS (352–366). The story is complicated, but the essentials can be told simply enough. The Arian emperor Constantius had, with typical Byzantine imperial arrogance, "deposed" Liberius in 355 for not subscribing to Arianism. After two years of exile, Liberius came to some kind of accord with the still Arian emperor, who then permitted him to return to Rome. What compromise doctrinal formula he signed or even whether he signed it is unknown (St. Hilary of Poitiers asserted that he had), but it is surely not without significance that Liberius, the thirty-sixth pope, is the only one among fifty-four popes from St. Peter to St. Gelasius I who is not revered as a saint in the West. At least in those days, popes were not automatically canonized, especially if they messed up on the job and failed to be the outstanding shepherds they should have been.

POPE VIGILIUS (537–555). The charges against Vigilius are four. First, he made an intrigue with the empress Theodora, who offered to have him installed as pope in return for his reinstating the deposed Anthimus in Constantinople.[6] Second, he usurped the papacy. Third, he changed his position in the affair of the Three Chapters (writings that were condemned by the Eastern bishops for going too far in an anti-Monophysite direction). Vigilius at first refused to agree to the condemnation, but when the Second Council of Constantinople confirmed it, Vigilius was prevailed on by imperial pressure to ratify the conciliar decree. It seems that Vigilius recognized the condemnation of the Three Chapters as problematic because it was perceived in the West as undermining the doctrine of the Council of Chalcedon but nevertheless allowed himself to be cajoled into doing so. Fourth, his wavering on this question and his final decision were responsible for a schism that ensued in the West, since some of the bishops of Italy refused to accept the decree of Constantinople. Their schism against both Rome and the East was to last for many years.

POPE HONORIUS I (625–638). In their efforts to reconcile the Monophysites of Egypt and Asia, the Eastern emperors took up the doctrine of Monothelitism, which proposed that, while Christ has two natures, He has only one will. When this was rejected by theologians as also heretical, the further compromise was advanced that, although Christ has two wills, they have nevertheless only "one operation" (hence the name of the doctrine, Monenergism). This, too, was false, but the patriarch of Constantinople made efforts to promote reunion by stifling the debate and forbidding discussion of the matter. In 634, he wrote to Pope Honorius seeking support for this policy, and the pope gave it, ordering that neither expression ("one operation" or "two operations") should be defended. In issuing this reply, Honorius disowned the orthodox writers who had used the term "two operations." More seriously, he gave support to those who wished to fudge doctrinal clarity to conciliate a party in rebellion against the Church.

---

6   Following (sometimes verbatim) Henry Sire's account in *Phoenix from the Ashes* (Kettering, OH: Angelico Press, 2015), 17-18. Vigilius did not carry through with the reinstatement of Anthimus—but only because the Emperor forbade it.

Fifteen years later, the Emperor Constans II published a document called the *Typos* in which he ordained precisely the same policy that Honorius had done. However, the new pope, Martin I, summoned a synod that condemned the *Typos* and upheld the doctrine of two operations. An enraged Constans had Martin brought to Constantinople and, after a cruel imprisonment, exiled him to the Crimea, where he died, for which reason he is revered as a martyr—the last of the papal martyrs (so far). In 680–681, after the death of Constans, the Third Council of Constantinople was held, which discarded the aim of harmony with the Monophysites in favor of that with Rome. Flaunting solidarity with the persecuted Martin, it explicitly and famously disowned his predecessor: "We decide that Honorius be cast out of the holy Church of God." The then reigning pope, Leo II, in a letter accepting the decrees of this council, condemned Honorius with the same forthrightness: "We anathematize Honorius, who did not seek to purify this apostolic Church with the teaching of apostolic tradition, but by a profane betrayal permitted its stainless faith to be surrendered." In a letter to the bishops of Spain, Pope Leo II again condemned Honorius as one "who did not, as became the apostolic authority, quench the flame of heretical doctrine as it sprang up, but quickened it by his negligence."[7]

POPE JOHN PAUL II (1978–2005). John Paul II designed the gathering of world religions in Assisi in 1986 in such a way that the impression of indifferentism as well as the commission of sacrilegious and blasphemous acts were not accidental, but in accord with the papally approved program. His kissing of the Koran is all too well known. He was thus guilty of dereliction in his duty to uphold and proclaim the one true Catholic Faith and gave considerable scandal to the faithful.[8]

POPES WHO TAUGHT SOMETHING HERETICAL, SAVORING OF HERESY, OR HARMFUL TO THE FAITHFUL

Here we enter into more controversial territory, but there can be no doubt that the cases listed below are real problems for a papal positivist or ultramontanist, in the sense that the latter term has recently acquired: one who overstresses the authority of

---

7   Again following the account in Sire, *Phoenix*, 18-19.
8   See Sire, *Phoenix*, 384-88.

the words and actions of the reigning pontiff as if they were the sole or principal standard of what constitutes the Catholic Faith.

POPE PASCHAL II (1099–1118). In his desire to obtain cooperation from Emperor Henry V, Pope Paschal II reversed the policy of all of his predecessors by conceding to the emperor the privilege of investiture of bishops with the ring and crosier, which signified both temporal and spiritual power. This concession provoked a storm of protest throughout Christendom. In a letter, St. Bruno of Segni (c. 1047–1123) called Pope Paschal's position "heresy" because it contradicted the decisions of many church councils and argued that whoever defended the pope's position also became a heretic thereby. Although the pope retaliated by removing St. Bruno from his office as abbot of Monte Cassino, eventually Bruno's argument prevailed, and the pope renounced his earlier decision.[9]

POPE JOHN XXII (1316–1334). In his public preaching from November 1, 1331 to January 5, 1332, Pope John XXII denied the doctrine that the just souls are admitted to the beatific vision, maintaining that this vision would be delayed until the general resurrection at the end of time. This error had already been refuted by St. Thomas Aquinas and many other theologians, but its revival on the very lips of the pope drew forth the impassioned opposition of a host of bishops and theologians, among them Guillaume Durand de Saint Pourçain, Bishop of Meaux; the English Dominican Thomas Waleys, who, as a result of his public resistance, underwent trial and imprisonment; the Franciscan Nicholas of Lyra; and Cardinal Jacques Fournier. When the pope tried to impose this erroneous doctrine on the Faculty of Theology in Paris, the king of France, Philip VI of Valois, prohibited its teaching and, according to accounts by the Sorbonne's chancellor, Jean Gerson, even reached the point of threatening John XXII with burning at the stake if he did not

---

9   Following the detailed account of Roberto de Mattei, "St. Bruno's Filial Resistance to Pope Paschal II," in *Love for the Papacy*, 35–39. It is true that the term "heresy" was used rather widely in earlier times, almost as shorthand for "anything that looks or sounds uncatholic," but there is implicit in Paschal II's temporary stance on investiture a false understanding of the true, proper, independent, divine, and non-transferable authority of the Church hierarchy vis-à-vis all temporal authority. It is, in other words, a serious matter, not a mere kerfuffle over bureaucratic procedure.

make a retraction. The day before his death, John XXII retracted his error. His successor, Cardinal Fournier, under the name Benedict XII, proceeded forthwith to define *ex cathedra* the Catholic truth in this matter. St. Robert Bellarmine admits that John XXII held a materially heretical opinion with the intention of imposing it on the faithful but was never permitted by God to do so.[10]

POPE PAUL III (1534-1549). In 1535, Pope Paul III approved and promulgated the radically novel and simplified breviary of Cardinal Quignonez, which, although approved as an option for the private recitation of clergy, ended up in some cases being implemented publicly. Some Jesuits welcomed it, but most Catholics—including St. Francis Xavier—viewed it with grave misgivings and opposed it, sometimes violently, because it was seen as an unwarrantable attack on the liturgical tradition of the Church.[11] Its very novelty constituted an abuse of the *lex orandi* and therefore of the *lex credendi*. It was harmful to those who took it up because it separated them from the Church's organic tradition of worship; it was a private person's fabrication, a rupture with the inheritance of the saints. In 1551, Spanish theologian John of Arze submitted a strong protest against it to the Fathers of the Council of Trent. Fortunately, Pope Paul IV repudiated the breviary by rescript in 1558, some 23 years after its initial papal approval, and Pope St. Pius V altogether prohibited its use in 1568. Thus, five popes and 33 years after its initial papal approval, this mangled "on the spot product" was buried.[12]

POPE PAUL VI (1963-1978). As the pope who promulgated all of the documents of the Second Vatican Council, whatever problems are contained in those documents—and these problems,[13]

---

10   For full details, see de Mattei, *Love for the Papacy*, 40-44.

11   See Alcuin Reid, *The Organic Development of the Liturgy: The Principles of Liturgical Reform and Their Relation to the Twentieth-Century Liturgical Movement Prior to the Second Vatican Council*, second edition (San Francisco: Ignatius Press, 2005), 37.

12   We should not be surprised to find that, almost four hundred years later, Archbishop Bugnini in 1963 expressed his unbounded admiration for the Quignonez Breviary, which in many ways served as the model for the new Liturgy of the Hours.

13   In *Phoenix from the Ashes*, Henry Sire provides excellent commentary on many of the difficulties of Vatican II. One may also profitably consult Roberto de Mattei, *The Second Vatican Council: An Unwritten Story* (Fitzwilliam, NH: Loreto Publications, 2021) and Bishop Athanasius Schneider, with Diane

neither insignificant nor few in number, have been identified by many—must be laid at the feet of Paul VI. One might, for example, point out materially erroneous statements in *Gaudium et Spes* (e.g., n. 24, which asserts that "love of God and neighbor is the first and greatest commandment,"[14] or n. 63, which asserts that

Montagna, *Christus Vincit: Christ's Triumph Over the Darkness of the Age* (Brooklyn, NY: Angelico Press, 2019), 117–35 et passim. Msgr. Bruno Gherardini has made excellent contributions: see Côme de Prévigny, "A Dark Cloud in the Conciliar Sky," *The Angelus Online*, June 2010. Paolo Pasqualucci has provided a list of twenty-six points of rupture: see "'Points of Rupture' of the Second Vatican Council with the Tradition of the Church—A Synopsis," *OnePeterFive*, April 13, 2018. While I do not agree with every point Pasqualucci argues, his outline is sufficient to show what a mess the Council documents are and what an era of unclarity they have prompted. The simple fact that popes over the past fifty years have spent much of their time issuing one "clarification" after another, usually about points on which the Council spoke ambiguously— one need only think of the oceans of ink spilled on *Sacrosanctum Concilium*, *Lumen Gentium*, *Dignitatis Humanae*, and *Nostra Aetate*—is sufficient to show that it failed in the function for which a council exists: to assist Catholics in knowing their faith better and living it more fully.

14   This contradicts Christ's own words: "'Love the Lord your God with all your heart and with all your soul and with all your mind.' *This is the first and greatest commandment*. And the second is like it: 'Love your neighbor as yourself.' All the Law and the Prophets hang on these two commandments" (Mt. 22:37–40). Are we required *both* to assent to Christ's words that the first and greatest commandment is the love of God while the second is love of neighbor *and* to assent to GS 24 that the first and greatest commandment is the love of God-and-neighbor (cf. *Apostolicam Actuositatem* 8)?

While the love of God and of neighbor are intimately conjoined, love of neighbor cannot stand on the same level as the love of God, as if they were the very same commandment with no differentiation. Yes, in loving our neighbor, we do love God, and we love Christ, but God is the first, last, and proper object of charity, and we love our neighbor *on account of* God. We love our neighbor and even our enemies *because* we love God more and *in a qualitatively different way*: the commandment to love God befits His infinite goodness and supremacy, while the commandment to love one's fellow man befits his finite goodness and relative place. If there were only *one* commandment of love, then we would be entitled to love God as we love ourselves—which would be sinful—or to love our neighbor with our whole heart, soul, and mind—which would also be sinful. In short, it is impossible for one and the same commandment to be given for the love of God and the love of neighbor.

The same erroneous view is found in Pope Francis's *Evangelii Gaudium* 161: "Along with the virtues, this [observance of Christ's teaching] means above all the new commandment, the first and the greatest of the commandments, "man is the source, the center, and the purpose of all economic and social life"[15]), but it is perhaps the Declaration on Religious Liberty *Dignitatis Humanae* (December 7, 1965) that will go down in history as the low water mark of this assembly. Like some kind of frenzied merry-go-round, the hermeneutical battles over this document will never stop until it is definitively set aside by a future pope or council. In spite of Herculean (and verbose) attempts at reconciling *DH* with the preceding magisterium, it is at least *prima facie* plausible that the document's assertion of a right to hold and propagate erroneous religious beliefs, even if they be misunderstood by their partisans as truth, is contrary both to natural reason and to the Catholic faith.[16]

Far worse than this is the first edition of the *General Instruction of the Roman Missal*, promulgated with the signature of Paul VI on April 3, 1969, which contained heretical statements on the nature of the Holy Sacrifice of the Mass. When a group of Roman theologians headed by Cardinals Ottaviani and Bacci pointed out the grave problems, the pope ordered the text to be corrected so that a second revised edition could be brought out. In spite of the fact that the differences in the text are astonishing, the first edition was never officially repudiated, nor was it ordered to be destroyed; it

---

and the one that best identifies us as Christ's disciples: 'This is my commandment, that you love one another as I have loved you' (Jn. 15:12)." Here John 15:12 has been taken for the *first and greatest* commandment, which it is not, according to Our Lord's own teaching. Characteristic of the same confusion are the misleading applications of Romans 13:8,10 and James 2:8 that follow in *EG* 161, which give the impression that "the law" being spoken of is comprehensive, when in fact it refers to the *moral* law. In other words, to say that love of neighbor "fulfills the whole law" means that it does all that the law requires in our dealings with one another. It is not speaking of our prior obligation to love God first and more than everyone else, including our very selves.

15   This might have been true in a hypothetical universe where the Son of God did not become man (although one might still have a doubt, inasmuch as the Word of God is the exemplar of all creation), but in the *real* universe of which the God-Man is the head, the source, and the center, the purpose of all economic and social life is and cannot be other than the Son of God, Christ the King, and, consequently, the realization of *His* Kingdom. Anything other than that is a distortion and a deviation. The fact that the same document says elsewhere that God is the ultimate end of man (e.g., *GS* 13) does not erase the difficulty in *GS* 63.

16   See Sire, *Phoenix*, 331-58, for an excellent treatment of the problems.

was merely replaced.[17] Moreover, although expounding the claim would exceed the scope of this article, the promulgation of the *Novus Ordo Missae* itself was both a dereliction of the pope's duty to protect and promote the organic tradition of the Latin Rite and an occasion of immense harm to the faithful.

POPE JOHN PAUL II asserted on multiple occasions a right to change one's religion, *regardless* of what that religion may be. This is true only if you hold to a false religion, because no one is bound to what is false, whereas everyone is bound to seek and adhere to the one true religion. If you are a Catholic, you cannot possibly have a right, either from nature or from God the author of nature, to abandon the Faith. Hence, a statement such as this: "Religious freedom constitutes the very heart of human rights. Its inviolability is such that individuals must be recognized as having the right even to change their religion, if their conscience so demands"[18] is false taken at face value—and dangerously false, one might add, because of its liberal, naturalistic, indifferentist conceptual foundation.

POPE FRANCIS. One hardly knows where to begin with this egregious doctor (and I do not mean it in the complimentary sense of *doctor egregius*). Indeed, an entire website called "Denzinger-Bergoglio" lists, in painstaking detail, all of the statements of this pope that have contradicted Sacred Scripture and the Magisterium of the Catholic Church. Nevertheless, we may identify several particularly dangerous false teachings.

(1) The explicit approval of giving Holy Communion to divorced and "remarried" Catholics who have no intention of living as brother and sister, expressed as a possibility in the post-synodal apostolic exhortation *Amoris Laetitia* and confirmed as a reality in the letter to the bishops of Buenos Aires published in the *Acta Apostolicae Sedis*.[19]

---

17   For details, see Michael Davies, *Pope Paul's New Mass* (Kansas City: Angelus Press, 2009), 299–328; Sire, *Phoenix*, 249, 277–82.

18   *Message for the World Day of Peace*, 1999. Compare the formula in a letter from 1980: "freedom to hold or not to hold a particular faith and to join the corresponding confessional community."

19   See John Lamont's penetrating study "The Meaning of *Amoris Laetitia* According to Pope Francis," in Lamont and Pierantoni, *Defending the Faith*, 215–33.

(2) The attempted change in teaching on capital punishment, first raised in a speech in October 2017 and now imposed on the Church by means of a change to the *Catechism*, in spite of the fact that the new doctrine manifestly goes against a unanimous tradition with its roots in Scripture.[20] The worst aspect of this change, as many have already pointed out, is that it loudly transmits the signal, most welcome to progressives, liberals, and modernists, that doctrines handed down over centuries or millennia, printed in every penny catechism that has ever rolled off the printing press, are up for revision, even to the point of saying the opposite, when the Zeitgeist pipes and the pope dances to the tune. There is no telling what further "development of doctrine" is in store for us enlightened moderns who see so much farther into the moral law than our barbaric predecessors. Ordination of females, overcoming the last vestiges of primitive patriarchalism? Legitimization of contraception and sodomy, finally letting go of the reductionistic biologism that has plagued Catholic moral teaching with the bugbear of "intrinsically disordered acts"? And so on and so forth.

As a Benedictine friend of mine likes to say: "The issue is not the issue." A Dominican priest perceptively wrote: "This isn't about the death penalty. It's about getting language into the *Catechism* that allows theologians to evaluate doctrine/dogma in historicist terms; that is, 'This truth is no longer true because times have changed.' The Hegelians got their wish."

(3) The annulment reforms, which amount, in practice, to an admission of "Catholic divorce" because of the novel concept of a "presumption of invalidity."[21]

---

20   See volume 2, chapters 13 and 14, and Ed Feser, "Pope Francis and Capital Punishment," *First Things*, August 3, 2018.

21   First, such a presumption contradicts both the natural moral law and the divine law. Second, even if there were nothing doctrinally problematic in the content of the pertinent motu proprios, the result of a vast increase in easily granted annulments on thin pretexts will certainly redound to the harm of the faithful by weakening the already weak understanding of and commitment to the indissoluble bond of marriage among Catholics, by making it much more probable that some valid marriages will be declared null (thus rubber-stamping adultery and profaning the sacraments), and by lowering the esteem with which all marriages are perceived. For good commentary, see Joseph Shaw's series of four articles: "Marriage and Annulment Reform," "Worries about the Arguments for Annulment Reform,"

This overview, from Paschal II to Francis, suffices to allow us to see one essential point: if heresy can be held and taught by a pope, even temporarily or to a certain group, it is *a fortiori* possible that disciplinary acts promulgated by the pope, even those intended for the universal Church, may also be harmful. After all, heresy in itself is worse than lax or contradictory discipline.

MELCHIOR CANO, AN EMINENT THEOLOGIAN AT THE Council of Trent, famously said:

> Now one can say briefly what [those do] who temerariously and without discrimination defend the supreme pontiff's judgment concerning everything whatsoever: these people unsteady the authority of the Apostolic See rather than fostering it; they overturn it rather than shoring it up. For . . . what profit does he gain in arguing against heretics if they perceive him as defending papal authority not with judgment but with emotion, nor as doing so in order to draw forth light and truth by the force of his argument but in order to convert another to his own thought and will? Peter does not need our lie; he does not need our adulation.[22]

Let us return to our point of departure. The Catholic faith is revealed by God, nor can it be modified by any human being: "Jesus Christ is the same yesterday and today and for ever" (Heb. 13:8). The pope and the bishops are honored servants of that revelation, which they are to hand down faithfully, without novelty and without mutation, from generation to generation. As St. Vincent of Lérins

---

"Annulment Reform and the Kasper Proposal," and "What Will We Make of Quickie Annulments?," *LMS Chairman*, September 14, 15, 16, and 18, 2015.
22   *Reverendissimi D. Domini Melchioris Cani Episcopi Canariensis, Ordinis Praedicatorum, & sacrae theologiae professoris, ac primariae cathedrae in Academia Salmanticensi olim praefecti, De locis theologicis libri duodecim* (Salamanca: Mathias Gastius, 1563), 197. This is often cited in a paraphrase: "Peter has no need of our lies or flattery. Those who blindly and indiscriminately defend every decision of the Supreme Pontiff are the very ones who do most to undermine the authority of the Holy See—they destroy instead of strengthening its foundations." (This is how it appears, e.g., in George Weigel, *Witness to Hope: The Biography of John Paul II* [New York: HarperCollins, 1999], 15.)

so beautifully explains, there can be growth in understanding and formulation, but no contradiction, no "evolution." The truths of the Faith, contained in Scripture and Tradition, are authentically defined, interpreted, and defended in the narrowly circumscribed *acta* of councils and popes over the centuries. In this sense, it is quite proper to say: "Look in Denzinger—that's the doctrine of the Faith."

Catholicism is, has always been, and will always be stable, perennial, objectively knowable, a rock of certitude in a sea of chaos—despite the efforts of Satan and his dupes to change it. The crisis we are passing through is largely a result of collective amnesia of who we are and what we believe, together with a nervous tendency toward hero-worship, looking here and there for the Great Leader who will rescue us. But our Great Leader, our King of Kings and Lord of Lords, is Jesus Christ. We follow and obey the pope and the bishops inasmuch as they transmit to us the pure and salutary doctrine of Our Lord and guide us in following His way of holiness, *not* when they offer us polluted water to drink or lead us to the muck. Just as Our Lord was a man like us in all things except sin, so we follow them in all things except sin—whether their sin be one of heresy, schism, sexual immorality, or sacrilege. The faithful have a duty to form their minds and their consciences to know whom to follow and when. We are not mechanical puppets.

Neither are the popes: they are men of flesh and blood, with their own intellect and free will, memory and imagination, opinions, aspirations, ambitions. They can cooperate better or worse with the graces and responsibilities of their supreme office. The pope unquestionably has a singular and unique authority on earth as the vicar of Christ. It follows that he has a moral obligation to use it virtuously, for the common good of the Church—and that he can *sin* by abusing his authority or by failing to use it when or in the manner in which he ought to do so. Infallibility, correctly understood, is the Holy Spirit's gift to him; the right and responsible use of his office is *not* something guaranteed by the Holy Spirit. Here the pope must pray and work, work and pray like the rest of us. He can rise or fall like the rest of us. Popes can make themselves worthy of canonization or of execration. At the end of his mortal pilgrimage, each successor of St. Peter will either attain eternal salvation or suffer eternal damnation. All

Christians, in like manner, will become either saintly by following the authentic teaching of the Church and repudiating all error and vice or damnable by following spurious teaching and embracing what is false and evil.[23]

I can hear an objection from some readers: "If a pope can go off the rails and stop teaching the orthodox Faith, then what's the point of having a papacy? Isn't the whole reason we have the vicar of Christ to enable us to know *for certain* the truth of the Faith?"

The answer is that the Catholic Faith *preexists* the popes, even though they occupy a special place vis-à-vis its defense and articulation. This Faith can be known with certainty by the faithful through a host of means—including, one might add, five centuries' worth of traditional catechisms from all over the world that concur in their teaching.[24] The pope is not able to say, like an absolute monarch: *La foi, c'est moi.*

But let us look at numbers for a moment. This article has listed eleven immoral popes and ten popes who dabbled, to one degree or another, in heresy. There have been a total of 266 popes. If we do the math, we come out with 4.14% of the Successors of Peter who earned opprobrium for their moral behavior and 3.76% who deserve it for their dalliance with error. On the other hand, about 90 of the preconciliar popes are revered as saints or blesseds, which is 33.83%. We could debate about the numbers (have I been too lenient or too severe in my lists?), but is there anyone who fails to behold in these numbers the evident hand of Divine Providence? A monarchy of 266 incumbents lasting for 2,000 years that can boast failure and success rates like this is no mere human construct, operating by its own steam.

These numbers teach us two lessons. First, we learn a sense of wonder and gratitude before the evident miracle of the papacy. We learn trust in a Divine Providence that guides the Holy Church of God through the tempests of ages and makes it outlast even the relatively few bad papacies we have suffered for our testing or for our sins. Second, we learn discernment and realism. On the one hand, the Lord has led the vast majority of His vicars along the way of truth so that we can *know* that our confidence is well placed in the barque of Peter, steered by the hand of Peter. Yet the

---

23   See chapter 12.

24   See www.whispersofrestoration.com/traditional-catechisms.

Lord has also permitted a small number of His vicars to falter or fail so that we will see that they are not automatically righteous, effortlessly wise in governance, or a direct mouthpiece of God in teaching. The popes must freely choose to cooperate with the grace of their office, or they, too, can go off the rails; they can do a better or worse job of shepherding the flock, and once in a while, they can be wolves. This happens rarely, but it does happen by God's permissive will, precisely so that we do not abdicate our reason, outsource our faith, and sleepwalk into ruin. The papal record is remarkable enough to testify to a well-nigh miraculous otherworldly power holding at bay the forces of darkness, lest the "gates of hell" prevail; but the record is speckled just enough to make us wary, keep us on our toes. The advice "be sober, be vigilant" applies not only to interactions with the world "out there," but to our life in the Church, for "our adversary, the devil, as a roaring lion, walketh about, seeking whom he may devour" (1 Pet. 5:8), from the lowly pewsitter to the lofty hierarch.

Our teacher, our model, our doctrine, our way of life: these are all *given* to us, gloriously manifested in the Incarnate Word, inscribed in the fleshy tablets of our hearts. We are not awaiting them from the pope, as if they do not already exist in finished form. The pope is here to *help* us to believe and to do what Our Lord is calling every one of us to believe and do. If any human being on the face of the Earth tries to stand in the way—be it even the pope himself—we must resist him and hold fast to what we know is right.[25] As the great Dom Prosper Guéranger wrote:

> When the shepherd becomes a wolf, the first duty of the flock is to defend itself. It is usual and regular, no doubt, for doctrine to descend from the bishops to the faithful, and those who are subject in the faith are not to judge their superiors. But in the treasure of revelation there are

---

25   St. Robert Bellarmine: "Just as it is licit to resist the Pontiff that aggresses the body, it is also licit to resist the one who aggresses souls or who disturbs civil order, or, above all, who attempts to destroy the Church. I say that it is licit to resist him by not doing what he orders and by preventing his will from being executed; it is not licit, however, to judge, punish, or depose him, since these acts are proper to a superior" (*De Romano Pontifice,* II.29, cited in Christopher Ferrara and Thomas Woods, *The Great Façade,* second ed. [Kettering, OH: Angelico Press, 2015], 187).

essential doctrines which all Christians, by the very fact of their title as such, are bound to know and defend. The principle is the same whether it be a question of belief or conduct, dogma or morals....The true children of Holy Church at such times are those who walk by the light of their baptism, not the cowardly souls who, under the specious pretext of submission to the powers that be, delay their opposition to the enemy in the hope of receiving instructions which are neither necessary nor desirable.[26]

---

26   *The Liturgical Year*, trans. Laurence Shepherd (Great Falls, MT: St. Bonaventure Publications, 2000), vol. 4, *Septuagesima*, 379–80. He is speaking here of opposition to the Nestorian heresy.

3
Portrait of a Perfect Pontiff

S IR FRANCIS GALTON (1822–1911), WHO MUST have been a rather interesting person to merit being described as a "statistician, polymath, sociologist, psychologist, anthropologist, eugenicist, tropical explorer, geographer, inventor, meteorologist, proto-geneticist, and psychometrician," believed that he could arrive at a forensically helpful composite portrait of the criminal type by combining many photographs until a certain standard face appeared. Of course a lot of his ideas were driven by Darwinist quackery, of the kind to which Victorian men of science seemed particularly vulnerable.

As implausible as this may sound, his photographic project did prompt me wonder if there might be a spiritual equivalent: could we establish a composite portrait of the Catholic Saint? Is there a certain "look" that would tell us: "this person is a saint"?

Acquaintance with hagiography puts the kibosh on such an enterprise. The saints are far too different from one another, in their inner character no less than in their external physiognomy. But I think one *could* get somewhere by working within categories: martyrs, virgins, widows, hermits, monks, doctors, kings and queens, and so forth.

What if, for example, we wanted a portrait of the ideal pope—the kind of Roman pontiff with whom God would be pleased? Where might we look for our raw materials? The thought occurred to me that the traditional *Roman Martyrology* (last edition 1956) would, in its succinct but often eloquent descriptions of eighty-three great popes, furnish us with the traits of papal greatness.[1]

---

1   The *Martyrology*, in English translation, is available either in deluxe hardcover from Angelus Press or as a compact paperback from Os Justi Press. The popes who are merely mentioned, with no description, give us no material to work with, so we will pass them by. They are St. Vitalian (Jan. 27), St. Hilarus (Feb. 28/29), St. Simplicius (Mar. 10), St. Soter (Apr. 22), St. Agapitus I (Apr. 22), St. Benedict II (May 8), St. John I (May 18/27), St. Felix (May 30/Dec. 30), St. Eugene I (Jun. 2), St. Paul I (Jun. 28), St. Leo II (Jul. 3), St. Leo IV (Jul. 17), St. Victor I (Jul. 28), St. Innocent I (Mar. 12/Jul. 28), St. Hormisdas (Aug. 6),

MARTYRS IN PAGAN ROME

A few popes are noted simply as martyrs under named Roman Emperors: St. Antherus (Jan. 3), St. Fabian (Jan. 20), St. Anicetus (Apr. 17), St. Caius (Apr. 22), St. Cletus (Apr. 26), St. Pius I (Jul. 11), St. Sixtus II (Aug. 6). Rather poetically, St. Evaristus (Oct. 26) is said to have "empurpled the Church of God with his blood under the Emperor Hadrian," while St. Telesphorus (Jan. 5) "attained an illustrious martyrdom under Antoninus Pius, after many labors in the service of Christ." St. Hyginus (Jan. 11) "gloriously consummated his martyrdom in the persecution of Antoninus," while, on the same day, St. Melchiades (Jan. 11/Dec. 10[2]) "suffered much in the persecution of Maximian, and, when peace had returned to the Church, fell asleep in the Lord." Sixtus I (Apr. 3) "ruled the Church with the greatest distinction in the reign of the Emperor Hadrian, and at last in the reign of Antoninus Pius willingly bore temporal death that he might gain Christ." St. Marcellinus (Oct. 25/Apr. 26) was beheaded in a persecution that took 17,000 Christian lives in one month. St. Callistus I (Oct. 14) "was long tortured by starvation in prison and scourged daily; lastly he was thrown from a window of the house wherein he was kept and drowned in a well, so meriting the triumph of victory."

EXILES FOR FIDELITY

In our times, many good priests have been forced into one or another form of ecclesiastical exile due to their commitment to orthodoxy and tradition. They should take comfort in the number of popes who suffered exile under their pagan overlords. St. Pontian (Oct. 30/Nov. 19) was exiled to Sardinia, where he died. St. Clement I (Nov. 23) "held the pontificate third after blessed Peter the Apostle, and in the persecution of Trajan was exiled to the Crimea. There an anchor was tied to his neck and he was cast into the sea and crowned with martyrdom." St. Cornelius (Sep. 14) "after being exiled . . . was commanded to be beaten with leaden scourges, and was beheaded with twenty-one others of both sexes."

St. Eusebius (Aug. 17), St. Sixtus III (Aug. 19), St. Zephyrin (Aug. 26/Dec. 20), St. Boniface I (Sep. 4), St. Sergius I (Sep. 8), St. Linus (Sep. 23), St. Mark (Oct. 7), St. Zosimus (Dec. 26).

2   If two dates are given in parentheses, it means the pope died on the first date but his feast or commemoration takes place on the second.

St. Lucius I (Mar. 4) "was sent into exile for the faith of Christ in the persecution of Valerian, and afterwards by the favor of God was permitted to return to his Church. When he had labored much against the Novatianists, he fulfilled his martyrdom by beheading."

WITNESSES IN SUFFERING

The pagan Romans were not the only ones to make life exceedingly difficult for popes. St. John I (May 18/27) was "lured to Ravenna by Theodoric, the Arian king of Italy, and for long afflicted there in prison on account of the orthodox faith, until he died." St. Leo III (Jun. 12) had a rough time of it as well: "his eyes were torn out and his tongue cut out by wicked men, but God miraculously restored them." St. Symmachus (Jul. 19), "worn out by long suffering at the hands of schismatical factions, passed to the Lord, famous for his holiness."

DISTINGUISHED FOR CERTAIN VIRTUES

Certain popes are singled out for special qualities. St. Agatho (Jan. 10) is said to have been "remarkable for his holiness and learning"; in like manner, St. Gelasius I (Nov. 21), "noteworthy for learning and holiness." St. Leo IX (Apr. 19) was "famous for praiseworthy virtues and miracles." St. Zachary (Mar. 22) "governed the Church of God with great watchfulness, and, renowned for his merits, rested in peace." Bd. Eugene III (Jul. 8) ruled a monastery "with great and praiseworthy holiness and prudence" and, after being elected pope, "governed the Universal Church in great sanctity." Bd. Benedict XI (Jul. 7), a Dominican, "in the short space of his pontificate wonderfully promoted the peace of the Church, the restoration of discipline, and the increase of religion." St. Felix IV (Sep. 22) "labored much for the Catholic faith." St. Nicholas I (Nov. 13) was "outstanding in apostolic vigor." St. Gregory III (Dec. 10) "departed for heaven renowned for his holiness and good works." St. Denis (Dec. 26) was "renowned for his many labors for the Church, and for his teaching of the faith."

HAMMERING THE HERETICS

The earlier mention of the Novatianists puts us in mind of the stalwart efforts of popes to rid the Church of error and put things to rights. St. Damasus I (Dec. 11) "condemned the heresiarch Apollinaris and restored Peter, Bishop of Alexandria, when he was compelled to flee." St. Julius I (Apr. 12) "greatly labored for the Catholic faith against the Arians, and after a distinguished career rested in peace, famed for his sanctity."

The popes were prepared to suffer rather than compromise on dogma. Of St. Silverius (Jun. 20) we read: "Having refused to restore the heretical Bishop Anthimus, who had been deposed by his predecessor, Pope Agapit, at the instance of the wicked Empress Theodora he was driven into exile by Belisarius, and there died, overcome with many labors, for the Catholic faith." St. Celestine I (Jul. 27) "condemned Nestorius, the Bishop of Constantinople, and put Pelagius to flight. By his command the holy General Council of Ephesus was also held against the same Nestorius." St. Siricius (Nov. 26), "famous for learning, piety and religious zeal . . . condemned various heretics and strengthened ecclesiastical discipline by his most salutary decrees."

St. Leo I (Nov. 10/Apr. 11) stands as one of the two popes who genuinely deserve the name "Great": "During his pontificate the holy Council of Chalcedon took place and in it he condemned, through his legates, Eutyches, and afterwards confirmed by his own authority the decrees of this Council. At length, after he had issued many ordinances and had written copiously, as a Good Shepherd deserving well of the Holy Church of God and of the entire flock of Christ, he rested in peace." St. Martin I (Sep. 16/Nov. 12) called together a Council at Rome to condemn the heretics Sergius, Paul, and Pyrrhus; as a consequence, the heretical Emperor Constans took him prisoner by guile, brought him to Constantinople, and exiled him to the Crimea, where he ended his days, "being worn out with his labors for the Catholic faith." Most famous of all, we have St. Pius V (May 1/5) of the Order of Preachers, who "zealously and successfully restored ecclesiastical discipline, stamped out heresies, and battled against the enemies of the Christian name" and "governed the Catholic Church in holiness of life and law."

SQUASHING THE SARACENS

Bd. Victor III (Sep. 16) "shed a fresh luster on the Apostolic See, and with God's help gained a famous victory over the Saracens." Bd. Urban II (Jul. 29) "was resplendent for his zeal for learning and religion, and aroused the faithful, signed with the sign of the cross, to recover the holy places of Palestine from the power of the infidels." The aforementioned St. Pius V instituted "the Feast of the Blessed Virgin Mary of the Rosary and the commemoration of St. Mary of Victory... to be kept yearly in memory of the glorious victory obtained on this same day in a naval battle by the Christians against the Turks, by the help of the same Mother of God." Pope Innocent XI commanded that "the Feast of the Most Holy Name of the Blessed Virgin Mary... should be celebrated [on Sep. 12] by reason of the famous victory obtained over the Turks at Vienna in Austria by the help of the Blessed Virgin."

GREAT EVANGELIZERS

Certain popes are distinguished for the part they played in "the Old Evangelization"—which is proved by conversions of individuals and entire nations to the Faith. Examples include St. Silvester I (Dec. 31), who "baptized the Emperor Constantine the Great, and confirmed the Council of Nicaea and, after many other deeds accomplished in holiness, rested in peace"; he may be considered the pope whom God chose to inaugurate the long rise of Christendom. There was Urban I (May 25), "by whose exhortation and teaching many persons (including Tibertius and Valerian) received the faith of Christ and for it suffered martyrdom. He himself also suffered much for God's Church in the persecution of Alexander Severus, and at length was crowned with martyrdom by decapitation." St. Eleutherius (May 26) "brought many Roman nobles to the faith of Christ" and "sent SS. Damian and Fugatius to Britain, where they baptized King Lucius, together with his wife and almost all his people."

Who could forget St. Gregory I (Mar. 12), "eminent Doctor of the Church, and Confessor, who for his famous life and for the conversion of the English to the faith, is called the Great, and surnamed the Apostle of the English"? His worthy successor St. Gregory II (Feb. 11) "strenuously withstood the impiety of Leo the Isaurian"—that would have been iconoclasm—"and sent St. Boniface to preach the Gospel in Germany."

HONORING THE SAINTS

Popes have been among the greatest devotees of relics and builders of shrines. St. Paschal I (Feb. 11) "raised many bodies of the holy martyrs from their tombs, and buried them with honor in various churches of the City [of Rome]." St. Boniface IV (May

8) "purged the Pantheon, the ancient temple of all the gods, and consecrated it in honor of our Lady and all holy martyrs in the reign of the Emperor Phocas" (see May 13). St. Damasus I, whom we met already in connection with Apollinaris, also "discovered many bodies of holy martyrs and adorned their tombs with verse inscriptions." St. Eutychian (Dec. 7) "buried 342 martyrs in diverse places with his own hand. He himself was joined to them and crowned with martyrdom under the Emperor Numerian."

PROMOTERS OF LIBERTY

This heading does not refer to Lady Liberty or any of the false idols of the Enlightenment; it refers to the liberty of the Catholic Church to exist everywhere on the face of the Earth and to exercise her rights and duties towards the human race and, in particular, towards the faithful. In this way St. Gregory VII (May 25) was "the upholder and most valiant defender of the liberty of the Church." Bd. Innocent V (Jun. 22) "labored with gentle prudence to protect the liberty of the Church and for concord among Christians." Towering above all others in this regard was St. Pius X (Aug. 20/Sep. 3), "unconquerable defender of the integrity of the faith and the liberty of the Church, and distinguished by his zeal for the spread of the faith."

LABORERS FOR UNITY

Bd. Gregory X (Jan. 10) held the Second Council of Lyons: "under him the Greeks were restored to the unity of the faith, discord among Christians healed, the recovery of the Holy Land begun. He deserved well of the Universal Church, which he governed in great holiness." St. Adrian III (Jul. 8) was likewise "famous for his zeal for the reconciliation of the Easterns to the Roman Church." Bd. Urban V (Dec. 19) "merited well of the Church by restoring the Apostolic See to Rome, arranging a union of the Greeks and Latins, and repressing infidels."

UNUSUAL QUALITIES

Merely a catalog (but *what* a catalog!), the *Martyrology* gives us relatively little information about each saint or blessed listed. Nevertheless, occasionally one reads entries that stand out for unusual content. It is no different with the popes.

St. Stephen I (Aug. 2), "in the persecution of Valerian, when soldiers came to take him while he was celebrating Mass, continued to the end before the Altar the mysteries he had begun, intrepid and unmovable, and was beheaded where he stood."

St. Deusdedit I (Nov. 8) attained "merit so great that he healed a leper of his leprosy by a kiss."

Notoriously—at least for the poet Dante, who placed him in hell for "making the great refusal"—St. Pietro da Morrone (May 19), also known as St. Peter Celestine, "who after being an anchorite was created Supreme Pontiff and took the name Celestine V...abdicated the popedom and led a religious life in the desert, whence, famous for virtues and miracles, he passed to the Lord."

We have St. Felix III (Mar. 1), "an ancestor of St. Gregory the Great, who relates of him that he appeared to his niece St. Tharsilla and called her to heaven."

St. Anastasius I (Dec. 19) is described as "a man of dire poverty and apostolic zeal. St. Jerome in his writings says that Rome did not deserve to possess him for long, for it was not fitting that the capital of the world should be cut off under such a pontiff; not long after his death Rome was captured and sacked by the Goths."

SO...WHAT ABOUT THE PORTRAIT?

Although we see a fair amount of diversity under which the popes are held up for praise by Holy Mother Church in her *Martyrology*, I think we can see strong patterns that show us what a good pope will typically look like.

First, and rather obviously—although nowadays, one has to spell out even the most obvious things!—a good pope has to be *holy*, which means, devoted to intense personal prayer and sound liturgical prayer and known for ascetical self-discipline. Popes who radically alter the traditional worship of the Church do not qualify.[3]

Second, a good pope will be learned in the law of the Lord, at least to the extent of being able to teach true doctrine with unambiguous clarity. He will not, therefore, indulge in verbose and ambiguous babbling on the most important subjects,[4] or irrelevant palavering on any and every secular subject under the sun.

---

3   See volume 2, chapter 57.
4   See volume 2, chapter 55.

Third, and following immediately from the preceding, a good pope will, on the one hand, encourage the preaching of the Catholic Faith to all the nations—*the Catholic Faith* and nothing else, and with the purpose of converting men to the one true Church, not entering into ecumenical or interreligious fraternal organizations— and, on the other hand, endeavor to condemn and stamp out heresy, reaffirming orthodox Catholic doctrine.

Fourth, he will work to reform and reestablish discipline in the Church. Given the tendencies of fallen human nature and the ravages of time, the Church is always in danger of falling apart at the seams and coming unstuffed. A good pope labors to replace the stuffing and repair the seams. In particular, as Martin Mosebach notes, reform means a "return to form," that is, a tightening up and restoration of good practice, not relaxation or indulgence.

Fifth, he will be unafraid of suffering persecution from the enemies of the Church for teaching and doing what is right. Nothing and no one—not even the EU or the UN—will make him compromise on the rights of God or the rights of the Church. This includes the right of Christ the King to the adherence of every human mind, the allegiance of every human heart, and a due and proper official *public* worship or divine *cultus*.

Sixth, he will defend and support the Church in times of invasion, persecution, famine, plague, or war, doing all in his power to ensure the continual availability of public worship and the sacraments. He will organize relief and military aid to Christians against Moslems or any groups that would threaten to overwhelm society, such as the globalist-environmentalist-socialist-Freemasonic-LGBTQ-etc. elite(s). He would urge Catholics to remain faithful at all costs and never to compromise on essentials with political rulers. He would remind the world that we are chastised by God for our sins and called to repentance.

To sum it all up: the good pope is one who so faithfully follows in St. Peter's footsteps that he could say to the Lord with full conviction: "Thou art the Christ, the Son of the living God . . . Lord, Thou knowest all things: Thou *knowest* that I love Thee" (Mt. 16:16; Jn. 21:17). And Christ would not have to rebuke him in these words: "Go behind me, Satan, thou art a scandal unto Me: because thou savourest not the things that are of God, but the things that are of men" (Mt. 16:23).

4

Have There Been Worse Crises Than This One?

D ON'T YOU HATE IT WHEN FELLOW CATH-
olics say to you: "The Church has faced crises worse
than this one before"?

You hate it because you know it's false. Of several popes who
flirted with heresy, only two seem to have crossed a line: Honorius
and John XXII. Honorius made one error in regard to Christology;
he did so in a letter to a bishop. And for this he was posthumously
anathematized and excommunicated as a heretic by an ecumenical
council and by several of his successors in the papacy.[1] John XXII
preached a false position about the beatific vision in a series of
sermons—an error that was immediately attacked by theologians
of his day. He retracted it on his deathbed.[2] Could anyone in his
right mind dream of comparing the versatile disaster of the Francis
papacy to either Honorius or John XXII?[3] It's like comparing
Stalin to mischievous Boy Scouts.

If you press your point, they might backtrack a little: "Well, at
least there have been other crises *comparable* to this one."

Without a doubt, the Arian crisis was exceedingly bad: for a
certain period, only a handful out of the hundreds of bishops of
Christendom were orthodox, concerning the very point that defines
Christianity. Yet today, the vast majority of the world's *thousands* of
bishops refuse to maintain major elements of Catholic tradition; fail
to preach the Ten Commandments, and even contradict them (think
of *Amoris Laetitia*); abandon the defense of consistency between the
universal ordinary Magisterium and the papal Magisterium (think
of the death penalty issue); renounce the proclamation of Christ as
the Son of God, the only Savior of mankind, and of the one true
Church that He founded (think of the direction ecumenism and

---

1   See Pierantoni, "Need for Consistency," in *Defending the Faith*, 235–51;
de Mattei, *Love for the Papacy*, 23–29.
2   See de Mattei, *Love for the Papacy*, 40–44.
3   See volume 2, chapter 37.

interreligious dialogue have taken). This is a collective madness, a wickedness in high places never before seen on such a scale. It's not just the Emperor who has no clothes on; it's the entire court—all his officials, too, in a sort of government of gymnosophists.

The current situation combines every earlier heresy. Arianism of varying shades is back in business; we see paganism, polytheism, and pantheism returning.[4] Paul VI had already allowed Protestantism, with Enlightenment rationalism and Romantic sentimentalism, to invade the sanctuary; since then these trends have seeped into every other area of the Church. Erastianism or the subordination of the Church to the secular State is assumed now as an unavoidable and unchallengeable norm.[5] What we have, in fact, is "the collector of all heresies"—Modernism—on full display.[6] We are indeed living in the worst, by far the worst, crisis the Church has ever seen, in twenty centuries of history.

Let me summarize the three principles of modern Catholicism:

#1. Always trust the experts.
#2. Always trust the hierarchy.
#3. Always trust the Zeitgeist.

And here are the three reasons why traditionalists "Just Say No":

---

4   A sign of how bad things are was how little reaction/discussion the "Protest Against Pope Francis's Sacrilegious Acts" received (text and signatories printed in Lamont and Pierantoni, *Defending the Faith*, 167–76). The "nothing to see here folks, move along" approach has become rather strained, not to say surreal. Regarding the October 4, 2019 ceremony in the Vatican Gardens, those involved either knew what was going to be done, or they did not know; either way they were at fault. Standing in a circle and then bowing in a circle does not look like Christian worship; add a bunch of pagan-looking objects on a blanket in the middle of the circle and a shamaness doing her stuff and the picture is complete. This is non-Christian, immanentist, naturalist, "closed circle" worship. There's this thing called "due diligence." If the organizers didn't know what was going to happen in front of hundreds of cameras, to be broadcast to the ends of the earth, they were guilty of seriously sinful negligence; and if they (or some of them at least) *did* know and didn't care about the impressions that would be given, they are guilty of paganism and syncretism. See volume 2, chapter 48.

5   See "It is time for civil disobedience in the name of fidelity to Christ," *LifeSiteNews*, January 4, 2021.

6   The Latin of *Pascendi Dominici Gregis* uses the expression "*omnium haereseon conlectum*," which is better translated "collector of all heresies" than as "synthesis of all heresies." See volume 2, chapter 62.

As to #1: The devastation wrought by the liturgical reform—now augmented by officially instituted lectresses and acolytesses for horizontal variety.

As to #2: The inadequacy, incoherence, and cowardice of the episcopal teaching of Catholic doctrine, compounded by waves of abuse scandals.

As to #3. The black Modernism of 120 years ago, and the scarlet Modernism of 60 years ago, do not amicably dispose us to the lavender Modernism of today.

The situation is horrible, yes. But we had to reach this nadir if the Church was ever to be rid of the lingering evil of Modernism and a remnant of the faithful was ever to find its way out. We must thank God for exposing the darkness, perversity, chaos, and cruelty of the Modernist agenda, which, like Satan himself, dresses up as an angel of light in order to deceive, if possible, even the elect (cf. 2 Cor. 11:14; Mt. 24:24). Our situation is apocalyptic because it is *revelatory*; what was hidden has been, is being, unveiled. The faithful of Christ who have been placed on earth at just this moment in history are *most beloved* to their Lord, who is calling them to remain faithful precisely when it is most difficult and most countercultural, even counterinstitutional.

The Church was permitted by God to drift into a papocentrism that we can see, with historical hindsight, to have been extremely dangerous and damaging. Catholics came to view the pope as a god on earth, a divine oracle who could never be wrong. Yet the ways in which Pius X, Pius XII, and Paul VI chose to exercise their authority regarding the liturgy—each more so than the one before—was nothing short of atrocious. We witnessed, first, the breviary wrenched from a 1,500-year tradition, then Holy Week from a 1,000-year tradition, and finally the Mass and all the other sacraments from the entire matrix of tradition. Pope Francis is the *reductio ad absurdum* of the view that the pope is in complete command of the Church and of its doctrine and life, rather than being a humble servant of the *depositum fidei*. In him, the ruptures of his predecessors, which in them coexisted uneasily with more traditional Catholic pieties, have found an unresisting and unmixed welcome.

Some have asked why I am not, by now, a sedevacantist. The reason should be evident from the foregoing. Sedevacantists embrace ultramontanism to the maximum.[7] They may *say* that they make all the necessary distinctions, but it seems to me that they expect popes who are always reliable, good, prudent, and trustworthy, who never seriously fail in the discharge of their exalted office. But now that we've had over a century of popes who are problematic from one point of view or another, in a growing crescendo, the sedes look pretty foolish to be clinging to pontiffs prior to John XXIII—warts, wrinkles, and all—while rejecting the past six popes universally recognized as such by all Catholics, clerical and lay, apart from minuscule pockets of denial. Here, too, we have a *reductio ad absurdum* of excessive veneration of the papacy. The idea that Our Lord would permit His Church to have no pope for sixty years, to be (as St. Thomas Aquinas would put it) visibly headless and therefore no longer sacramentally conformed to the Mystical Body with its heavenly Head, seems far more absurd to me than questioning the earlier ultramontanism summed up in the exaggerated reception of Vatican I,[8] even as the execution and implementation of Vatican II summed up the soft modernism of the mid-twentieth century.[9]

It is more realistic, more in accord with the truth, to accept that popes can be wrong, can be imprudent and bad, as Church history has shown,[10] and that there are times when, as Roberto de Mattei demonstrates in his book *Love of the Papacy and Filial Resistance to the Pope in the History of the Church*, the proper Catholic response is to resist the evil that a valid pope is attempting to do, enforce, or permit. Anna Silvas incisively observes:

---

7   See chapter 15.

8   This is what I meant, obviously, when I used the expression "spirit of Vatican I" in "The Second Vatican Council Is Now Far Spent," *OnePeterFive*, December 11, 2019.

9   The fear of doctrinal definition and of anathemas that characterizes Vatican II—the first council in the history of the Church that would *not* define anything or condemn anything in a definitive way—has remained with us as a kind of paralysis. It is profoundly unpastoral not to teach the truth clearly and not to condemn clearly what is false or sinful. Again, the Church has *never* had *this* problem in 2,000 years, so something very basic has "snapped." It's not the indefectibility of the Church that has snapped, but the fidelity of her ministers to their roles. It is like being on a sturdy ship that is either unpiloted or being taken to the wrong port.

10   Admittedly, never to the extent we are witnessing, and yet the principle stands.

Eventually the Church, in a searching examination of conscience, must look again at the papacy itself, and what has been made of it, affectively. To return to the antinomies of the early 15th century is not possible—spare us from "synodality"—but some sober advance, surely, is needed. Related to this may be an examination of the influence of Jesuit/Ignatian ideas of obedience in the Tridentine era. By what strange symmetry, and *why*, did the proponents of a hyper-papal obedience (or any sort of religious hyper-obedience) end by becoming cheerleaders of dissent and disobedience? The one stance is not unrelated to the other. It turns our minds to the phenomena of "short-cuts" both in the Tridentine and post-Vatican II era Church. "Short-cuts"? Yes, *efficiency*, perhaps even *impatience,* a particular note of modernity.

St. Basil the Great came to close quarters (beginning with the 360 Council of Constantinople) with the terrible sickness of the Church, and in particular bishops' synods, in his day. It unnerved him terribly, and he personally had a crisis. Eventually he articulated a nuanced and yet clear teaching of when it becomes necessary to disobey the disobedient. And part of that process is mustering enough spiritual fortitude to face malfeasant superiors and communities, hoping in the first place for their conversion. What helps preserve us in the obedience of the faith is the internalisation of the *paradosis* in its fullest sense, safe-guarded above all in prayer and charity; I would put the sensibility of the Holy Liturgy, in essence the *Mystery of Christ,* at the heart of this comprehensive "net" of tradition.[11]

When Jesus says to the first pope: "Thou art Peter; and upon this rock I will build my church, and the gates of hell shall not prevail against it" (Mt. 16:18), he is not saying: "Don't worry, the devil will bounce off whenever he tries to strike, and all will be well." Rather, we should take Him at His word: on the one hand, the Church will prove stronger than hell in the end, no matter how fearsomely the devil rages and ravages; on the other hand, anything and everything short of total defeat and dissolution is

---

11   From personal correspondence.

fair game. It is when all appears to be lost that the Church will be resurrected. The clarity of this "logic," which mirrors that of the life of Christ,[12] becomes sharper and brighter as history proceeds irresistibly to the advent of "the lawless one," Antichrist, and of the Lord who will slay him with the breath of his mouth (cf. 2 Thess. 2:8).

The disciples on the road to Emmaus thought they were looking at total defeat: "But we had hoped that he was the one to redeem Israel" (Lk. 24:21). All appeared to be lost. So must it have seemed for a time at Lepanto. And when Our Lady says: "*In the end* my Immaculate Heart will triumph," how much force do we place on the phrase "*in the end*"? The bitter end—when it seems to be *the* end of our hopes, *the* end of the divine promises, *the* end of the fidelity of Rome: "When the Son of Man comes, will he find faith on earth?" (Lk. 18:8). "For there shall arise false Christs and false prophets, and shall shew great signs and wonders, insomuch as to deceive, if possible, even the elect" (Mt. 24:24). "Beloved, do not be surprised at the fiery trial when it comes upon you to test you, as though something strange were happening to you" (1 Pet. 4:12).

In short, a full meltdown of the Church on earth—which has always been a possibility given the logic of the Faith and the witness of the Scriptures—is taking place in front of our eyes, an apparent defeat and dissolution under the global assault of the Evil One, exactly as we should expect to occur at some point in the history of the Church. Whether we are already in the early phases of *the* end beyond which there is no more time is impossible to say. If we are not in the end times but rather passing through an advance echo of them, we may nevertheless say with confidence that it will take a "purgatory" of hitherto inconceivable catastrophes to restore the Catholic Church on earth to some semblance of sanity, in which the excesses inaugurated by the last two councils will be purged from the bloodstream of the body, and a healthier, humbler, more orthodox *Ecclesia* will emerge—like gold and silver seven times refined.

---

12   See "Christ's Life is the Church's Life," *New Liturgical Movement*, March 26, 2018.

5

The Church Never Fails—
but Churchmen Are
Another Story

I T IS WHEN THINGS ARE LOOKING BLEAKEST,
humanly speaking, that the act of faith in God's revelation
is most valuable and saving.

When the Church is sailing along in splendor and sanctity, and
when a culture is dominated by the Faith, one's religious life can
be carried along fairly effortlessly from cradle to tomb.

But then there are the times of crisis, when the surrounding
culture turns against the Church, when the Church's leaders
become corrupt, when charity grows cold among the faithful. At
such times it becomes harder to believe that the Church, in her
inmost nature as the Mystical Body of Christ, is His immaculate
Bride, spotless, sinless, totally united to Him—and that we need
to remain a part of this Church if we want to be saved.

The Church that is our mother, perfect Bride of Christ, the
heavenly Jerusalem (Gal. 4:26, Heb. 12:22, Rev. 21:9-10), is the city
we aspire someday to be permanent citizens of. The Church on
earth, however, is made up of wheat *and* weeds, the good and the
bad, the holy and the perverse—and lots of us who are straddling
the fence in between. Echoing St. Augustine, the great theologian
Emile Mersch observes:

> The source of sin remains in the Church militant in general,
> for what baptism does in the individual, the death of Christ
> has done for the whole Mystical Body. The Church is made
> up of sinners; hence her great prayers are the prayers of
> sinners, "Forgive us our trespasses"; "Holy Mary, Mother of
> God, pray for us sinners." Sin is in the Church, contagious
> and ineradicable, like the weeds in the field that are forever
> obstinately encroaching, and it will not be exterminated
> until the Church militant herself is no more, on the Last
> Day, the day of the harvest. The holiness of the Church

is not less real for all that, but it is realistic holiness, the sanctity of the Church militant. The Church is holy by reason of what God has placed and wrought in it, but it is not holy because of what men contribute of their own resources or because of the activity they perform in it so far as that activity proceeds from them alone.[1]

Jacques Maritain makes an important distinction between the "person" of the Church and her "personnel," which parallels Cardinal Journet's distinction between "the Church" and "churchmen."

On the one hand, the Church that Christ founded, the Church we belong to and in which we are saved, the *una sancta*—this is the one and only Church: the communion of orthodox and charity-filled believers with the Son of the living God, through the mysteries of the holy Eucharist and the other sacraments, kept alive in communities of apostolic succession. *This* Church can never fail, because Christ can never fail, nor will He fail those who are united to Him in the true faith, the hope of eternal life, and love for God and neighbor.

On the other hand, the *human representatives* of this Church, her temporary leaders on earth, who may be called "the Church" only in a limited sense, do falter and fail. They can fail their Lord; they can fail their people. They have received an objective office and the pledge of God's help, but they must subjectively cooperate with God's grace in order to fulfill their duties in a holy and God-pleasing manner. God alone is unchanging and unfaltering; until we attain heavenly beatitude, we are fickle, mutable, and in danger of corruption. All the more reason to cry out: "Save us, Lord, for we perish!"

However much they may wage war against everything that is sacred and true, no bishop, priest, deacon, or layman can take away from us the true faith, the hope of eternal life, and love for God and neighbor. These are God's gifts to us in His holy Church. As Jesus says in His priestly prayer, the Father has given the disciples into His hands, and no one can take them away; when the Father draws a soul into the ambit of His Son, the world cannot stall or stop Him from doing so. Nothing in all creation can separate us from the love of Christ (Rom. 8:35–39).

---

1   Emile Mersch, S. J., *The Theology of the Mystical Body,* trans. Cyril Vollert, S. J. (St. Louis: B. Herder, 1951), 308.

The *unum necessarium,* the one thing we need, is to sit at the feet of Christ, soak in His light and His truth, receive the gift of Himself, and give ourselves to Him in return. We know, or rather, we sincerely believe and hope, that in this way we are members of the one and only Church that exists in time, the one and only Church that exists in eternity. And there, in heaven, where alone the Church has her most perfect being, there is no reigning pope, no bishop, no sacraments, no temple (cf. Rev. 21:22)—nothing but the King of Kings in His unspeakable beauty, followed, loved, and adored for all eternity. *That* is the Mass we want to attend, and for its sake, we are willing to endure anything that the devil can sling at us, or better, that the Lord permits in His Providence.

AROUND THE TIME OF THE LETTER ACCUSING POPE Francis of heresy, I published an article entitled "When Creeping Normalcy Bias Protects a Chaotic Pope."[2] A reader wrote a letter to me that, I am sure, will resonate with many Catholics who are looking at the darkening situation and wondering: "How can it be happening that the pope is deviating from the Faith? Where am I to turn for guidance, if not the successor of St. Peter? Are Christ's promises crumbling? Is it hopeless?" Here is the reader's letter:

> At the end of your article, you quote a friend commenting on the Church's current crisis of truth and the final trial resulting in "washing away the petrified filth of vice and error and restoring [the Church] to her lost beauty." You then encourage your readers to "hold fast to the Catholic faith and pray more fervently than ever." My question is this: What do you mean by "the Catholic faith"? What does it translate into? People in the hierarchy as well as teachers, etc., mean very different things by this phrase. I'm even more concerned because you earlier state in the article "But to think the current crisis of Pope Francis can be contained by means of a few pat 'Catholic Answers' is like trying to extinguish the flames of Notre Dame with a squirt gun." While I don't disagree, this statement places me on a more uncertain foundation. What does it mean to hold fast to the Faith especially if "pat" Catholic answers are entirely

2   This text may be found in Lamont and Pierantoni, *Defending the Faith,* 379–83.

62

insufficient? I work in a parish and try to pass on the Faith.
Thanks for your efforts to let the truth shine forth.

I share my reply for the benefit of others who may find themselves
in the same mental anguish and impasse.

DEAR N.,

Yes, this is the burning question of our time: What *is* the
Catholic Faith? Is it simply infinitely malleable in the hands of
popes, councils, theologians? Or is there some way we can know
with rock-solid certainty that we are holding to "the faith delivered
once for all to the saints," as the Letter of Jude puts it?

The main thing I've noticed in my life is that a vast number of
people have little or no knowledge of the Faith beyond the Vatican
II era; they pay attention only to what has happened or been said
in the past sixty years. Ratzinger frequently criticized this move as
making Vatican II into a "Super-Council" that trumped everything
before, as if the Church were born in the 1960s. In reality, the
Faith is immeasurably vast and deep, and has two thousand years
of tradition behind it and within it—more like four thousand years,
if one includes Israel. This is the basic reason I'm a traditionalist:
not because I want to "go back" to a particular time in history, but
simply because I desire to embrace the sum-total of *all* of that history,
which is our birthright. I want to live from the totality, the fullness,
the whole, not from fragments, shells, and scraps. The tradition has
time-tested strength, solidity, resilience, coherence, subtlety, breadth;
the new version, "catholicism lite," has an abysmal record of fragility,
porousness, flimsiness, incoherence, brazenness, and narrowness.

More concretely: dozens of popes, an impressive sequence from
the thirteenth century to nearly the present, have recommended
the study of St. Thomas Aquinas. He is a safe guide in philosophy
and theology. For that reason, faithful Thomists like Frank Sheed,
Josef Pieper, and Fulton Sheen will also be safe guides.

Again, catechisms—which by definition are designed to transmit
the orthodox Faith in the simplest, clearest, most reliable manner—
were not born with the *Catechism of the Catholic Church*. There were
hundreds of catechisms before it, all published with the approval of
bishops; these may be seen as a collective witness to the universal
ordinary magisterium of the Church, which is infallible. The
most authoritative of these was the *Catechism of the Council of Trent*,

promulgated by Pope St. Pius V. Pope St. Pius X also published his own catechism. These two make for excellent resources on a catechetical level, as in: what do Catholics actually believe? *All* catechisms before now concurred with one another, whereas our current CCC, as modified by Francis on the death penalty, stands outside of this consensus. It is for reasons like this that I oppose Francis's errors: one does not simply cancel out the agreement of hundreds of catechisms spanning a 500-year period.[3] It is for similar reasons that I object to the liturgical reform: it likewise canceled out *centuries* of organic liturgical development.[4]

Like Christ, their Master, the preconciliar popes "teach with authority": you can see it in the clarity of their arguments, the unanimity of their conclusions, and the force of their proofs from Scripture and Tradition. I became Catholic, in a sense, by reading the encyclicals of Leo XIII, Pius X, Pius XI, and Pius XII. Once you cut your teeth on stuff like this, many later documents look mushy, verbose, confused, and afraid to say the truth. Not that they are positively false, but they become, in a way, uncertain of themselves. And this, in a nutshell, is the problem: the loss of the conviction of the truth and the evangelical missionary zeal that follows from it. We are in full meltdown because we have let go of the non-negotiable primacy of truth, the love for immortal souls and their salvation, and zeal for Christ the King and His Kingdom.

I think we can be quite confident that Our Lord does not want His Church to go into a period of self-doubt, self-denial, and self-psychoanalysis. This is an unhealthy introspection, a turning-inward that leaves us constantly second-guessing ourselves. We ask for bread and we seem to be getting stones, or maybe particolored pebbles. But the bread is there in the pantry of Catholic Tradition; it's there for the taking. Our Lord stocked it well, and gave it the miraculous property of never running out.

Cordially yours in Christ,
Peter Kwasniewski

---

3   See volume 2, chapter 40.
4   See my lecture "Beyond 'Smells and Bells': Why We Need the Objective Content of the *Usus Antiquior*," *Rorate Caeli*, November 29, 2019.

6

The State of the Church and the State of Our Souls

CATHOLICS STRIVING TO BE LOYAL TO "the faith once delivered to the saints" (Jude 1:3) are rightly and reasonably concerned about the state of the Church today. Things are looking bleak on many levels. Those who have eyes to see and ears to hear can see it and hear it in technicolor and surround-sound.

Obviously, we need to keep our eyes open to scope out the evils that threaten us and to watch where we're going—not merely to preserve ourselves from harm but to guide and protect all who depend on us. We need to keep our ears open, lest we fail to cling to the divine truth handed down to us by the Church of all ages and fail to notice the glaring discrepancies between that truth and the popular false gospels, including, sometimes, those preached by prelates. We have a duty to proclaim the full truth and bear witness to it in a holy manner of life.

People will have disagreements, it has always been so: look at the stern rebuke of Peter by Paul (Gal. 2:11) or the sharp contention between Paul and Barnabas (Acts 15:39). But rebukes and contentions can be done in different ways—in ways that build up, and in ways that tear down.

I

THE TIMES IN WHICH WE LIVE CONFRONT US SIMULtaneously with immense spiritual danger and opportunity for heroic virtue.

At the root level, in the custody of our inmost thoughts and desires, we must not allow *anything,* no matter how grievous, to distract us from gazing in our hearts on the face of Jesus Christ. If we are drawn into an excessive focus on the sins and errors of churchmen, we are not victors but losers, since we are led away from the only source of victory, Our Lord Himself, who is the sole measure of reality, the one consolation to the wandering pilgrim.

A sign that we are paying such things excessive attention would be a steady attitude of discouragement, which, as St. Thérèse taught in her simple way, is a form of pride, because it manifests how we are trusting in men, in ourselves, for salvation rather than in the God who alone saves. Other signs might include long-standing depression, *acedia* or spiritual lethargy, simmering anger, the disgusted abandonment of religious practice, or the approval of rebellious attitudes and actions on the part of those who are resisting the crisis in the Church. In the name of fidelity to tradition—a fidelity entirely laudable towards a good entirely lovable—we can so easily be deceived or deceive ourselves if we are not careful to keep our minds and hearts resting where they need to rest.

There is no deception or self-deception possible when one gives total obedience and loyalty to the Church on earth—as long as one understands what the proper object of this obedience and loyalty is. The object of supernatural faith, the theological virtue of faith, is God the Revealer and Him alone, *not* any mere human, not even the pope or bishops together in council. The content of the faith is what God has revealed and what He teaches on faith and morals through the Magisterium of His Church, when that authority is unmistakably engaged. Whatever teaching on faith and morals is promulgated by the pope to the entire Church, with the express engagement of his apostolic authority as successor of Saint Peter, all this we embrace with joyful obedience, knowing that neither Christ nor His Vicar, acting precisely as such, can deceive or be deceived.

All the same, as a Catholic I do not place my faith in the *pope* as such, but in *Christ* who teaches us through His ministers. If the pope (or any other bishop or cleric) should falter in the day-to-day preaching or living out of the Faith, my own faith remains unshaken; why should it be shaken? Christ is the immovable rock on which the Church is founded, and the pope is that rock precisely when and as he speaks and acts in communion with Christ. The pope, like all of reality, is subject to a measure outside himself—he is not himself the ultimate measure. It is the glory of the Catholic Faith that nothing we are bound to believe, nothing that is essential to our sanctification, is based on human whims or subjective opinions. Put the other way around, nothing based on human whims or subjective opinions will ever be among the articles of faith or the elements of sanctity. And if, to take the extreme case, something is stated or done by a prelate that conflicts with already-established doctrine on faith and morals, we know *ipso facto* that it has no other force than that of bad example.

Far too many people today, including apparently senior members of the hierarchy, seem to have forgotten the time-honored principle that there are many levels of authority at which a pope speaks, as gauged by the language he uses, the instrument in which the language appears, the occasion chosen, the reiteration of a teaching, and other such signs. It is also universally accepted that the pope can be mistaken in judgments of fact and prudential decisions, whenever faith and morals are not immediately and directly at stake. In other words, if I say "the Mass is not a true and proper sacrifice," I am *doctrinally* wrong, but if I say "attendance of Catholics at Mass in Europe is rapidly increasing" or "the abandonment of Latin brought more Catholics to Mass than ever before," I am *factually* wrong. This latter kind of statement simply is not doctrinal, nor, as a result, something to which a pope's infallibility could ever extend. In this sense, why would anyone doubt that a pope can say foolish things—don't we all? Man does not live by every word that comes from the mouth of the pope, but only those which come from the mouth of God; and the pope's words are those of God only when, and only because, he teaches authoritatively on faith and morals as the Vicar of Christ.

A further distinction can be granted, too: some teachings are timeless, while others are time-bound. The time-bound are binding so long as the circumstances for which they are intended remain. Of course, only the Church herself can indicate definitively that, in her judgment, the circumstances no longer obtain; and yet there are times when history has done this work for us, without any official judgment being necessary. Fr. Hunwicke has pointed out that many passages in Vatican II documents (*Gaudium et Spes* comes particularly to mind) now read like dated period-pieces, quaint with the naïve optimism of their day, perhaps even quaint at the moment they first appeared, and rapidly aging like the architectural products of the same period, which today are frequently torn down to make room for more beautiful and traditional buildings. Just as the passage of time condemned to irrelevance many thundering provisions of medieval councils, so, too, something like this is happening slowly to the Vatican II documents, or at least to their purple passages.

II

IT IS NOT THE CHURCH'S BUSINESS TO MAKE HER-
self pleasing and "understandable" to the world, if this will only
corrupt her saving message and her supernatural mission. It would
be like a woman prostituting herself in order to reach hardened
sinners. The truth of the faith takes precedence over a misty-eyed
camaraderie that so often degenerates into a weak-kneed surrender.
Rather, in her beauty, in her simplicity, in her unchanging doctrine,
the Church has the perennial power to attract even the worst
sinners, the most jaded or ideological intellectuals, Protestants,
Jews, unbelievers of every stripe.

The fundamental flaw with the Second Vatican Council can
be expressed quite simply: *aggiornamento* (updating) was taken as
a comprehensive program, and the program was taken in the
direction of the Church adapting itself to the world. Thus Louis
Bouyer speaks of "the temptation... of a false modernity, of a so-
called adaptation to modern needs which actually causes the loss
of true tradition as the result of an idolatry of ephemeral fashion,
and as a result of the unregulated fancies of individuals."[1] It was
thought that the Church—*the Church!*—needed "updating," when it
was really modernity that needed to be rescued from the tyranny
of the temporal, the illusion of progress, the vanity of humanism,
and the idolatry of technics. It was said that the Church's liturgy
no longer spoke to modern man, when in fact this was the *principal*
thing modern man lacked and needed to be initiated into. So
the Church was "updated," and threw off her past like the nuns
who threw off their habits or the parishes that tore down their
sanctuaries. The liturgy was redesigned in accommodation to the
spirit of the times. This "spirit" was misread; for the spirit of
our times is largely a diabolic spirit which can deceive even the
elect, as our Lord warns us (Mt. 24:24). So much of the Church's
internal activity since the Council has been the foolish (not to say
scandalous and destructive) effort to race forward, keeping pace with
the West as it plummets into the worst darkness that mankind has
ever known. As John Senior put it back in the 1970s:

---

1   *Liturgical Piety* (Notre Dame, IN: University of Notre Dame Press, 1955),
40. Whatever else he is, Bouyer is highly quotable. I do not, however, endorse
the predominantly anti-medieval and anti-Baroque sentiments of this book.

There is little comfort in the visible Church now. The liturgy, set upon by thieves, is lying in the ditch; contemplatives are mouthing political slogans in the streets; nuns have lost their habits along with their virtues, virgins their virginity, confessors their consciences, theologians their minds.

What is needed is something very like a new Counter-Reformation—only with this difference: that it must be a Counter-*Conciliarism*. For whether or not the Second Vatican Council can be blamed or implicated for any of the problems mentioned—a question on which scholarly debate continues to develop as people's minds thaw to admit a larger range of possibilities—nevertheless it is patently obvious, as Cardinal Ratzinger/Pope Benedict discussed many times, that the "spirit of the Council," in the name of which the most enormous atrocities and the most disgusting absurdities have been and still are committed, is clearly at the center of the crisis. To continue to "implement" the Council in the ways in which this implementation has been understood in the past sixty years will produce only more confusion, more loss of faith, more liturgical aberration, more impoverishment, more betrayal.

The contemporary liturgy, in part reflecting the condition of the Church and in part causing it, shares in this Western darkness, in its loss of the sacred, loss of the numinous. All too often, liturgies express not "the unsearchable riches of Christ" (Eph. 3:8) but the banality and (an-)aesthetic poverty of the West. That is why the restoration of the traditional liturgy is the most urgent apostolic mission of all, the antidote to a conciliar "implementation" by which countless Catholics have been alienated, superficialized, and compromised. The traditional liturgy has the power to turn the clock *forward* to an age of rediscovered light; the present liturgy has power only to keep us stuck in the ersatz theology of the '60s and '70s, with its inverse missiology (meaning: its anti-evangelical effects). The West needs to be re-evangelized, as the popes have insisted again and again; but does not evangelization demand, by its very nature, the *fullness* of liturgy reverently celebrated and the *fullness* of faith boldly proclaimed? There *is* no other evangelization, old or new, that is worthy of the name. The mysteries *are* the mission.

As the world goes down, the Church must raise her head again above the confusion and remain the beacon of light she has always been. That means *you and I* must be those beacons of light, working with God's grace to make of ourselves worthy Catholics who pray as the Church prayed before the changes, believe what she has always believed, and practice what her saints practiced. In this way we join the ranks of the Church of all times and places, making the Way, the Truth, and the Life present in the world and available to our neighbors. We must be agents of a "New Evangelization" that is new precisely because it newly reintroduces other Catholics, other Christians, and unbelievers—men and women utterly cut off from their roots—to the greatness of Tradition, ever ancient, ever new. This greatness is genuinely good news, with power to convince and convert. It is not the "Novel Evangelization" that we so often see, where novelty replaces substance, but a solid preaching of the Gospel, the whole, demanding, consoling, wondrously mysterious Gospel that feels fresh and new after the staleness and datedness of the past half-century.

As I said: the times in which we live confront us with, simultaneously, immense spiritual danger and opportunity for heroic virtue. Let us do what we can today, and every day, to dodge those dangers and seize those opportunities, for this is the making of saints.

7

On Keeping to Arduous Paths and Leaving Satan Behind

I HAVE DEVELOPED AN AFFECTION FOR A verse in Psalm 16: *Propter verba labiorum tuorum ego custodivi vias duras,* "On account of the words of Thy lips, I have kept the arduous paths" (Ps. 16:4). King David, to whom these words are attributed, knew what it was like to keep to arduous paths. At the low point of his reign, he was driven forth from his royal city by his usurping son Absalom.

> And David said to his servants, that were with him in Jerusalem: "Arise and let us flee: for we shall not escape else from the face of Absalom: make haste to go out, lest he come and overtake us, and bring ruin upon us, and smite the city with the edge of the sword." ... But David went up by the ascent of mount Olivet, going up and weeping, walking barefoot, and with his head covered, and all the people that were with them, went up with their heads covered weeping.... "Perhaps the Lord may look upon my affliction, and the Lord may render me good for the cursing of this day." (2 Sam. 15:14,30; 16:12)

We may not ever face a situation as desperate as the one faced by David, but no life will pass without its moments of weeping, affliction, and ruin. Some will be called to enter even more fully into the Passion of Christ and His martyrs. No matter what, we will be asked to tread arduous paths for the sake of God's Word.

MAKE FIRM MY STEPS IN THY WAYS

We learn from Scripture that the "arduous paths" for all of us are primarily two: the keeping of God's commandments and the offering of worthy worship to His divine Majesty. These things, which for unfallen man would have been easy and a source of delight, have become burdensome for fallen human nature. Christ our Lord has come to Earth, has given for us His very life and death, to restore some measure of ease and joy to those arduous paths by which we reach our ultimate destiny in the heavenly Jerusalem. "Take up my yoke upon you, and learn of me," He says, "because I am meek, and humble of heart: and you shall find rest for your souls" (Mt. 11:29-30).

This rest we find most of all in the Sacred Liturgy, where, like the cherubim, we "set aside all earthly cares" and throw ourselves into the infinite mystery of Jesus Christ. He alone can save us from our sins and from the Evil One who desires nothing more than to see us abandon the Faith, grow relaxed in our practice of it. When the Holy Sacrifice of the Mass is not available to us, we retreat into the Divine Office, the prayers of the Mass read from a missal or viewed from afar, the rosary, and other devotions. We hold on to the day of rest that Christ hallowed by His Resurrection:

> There remaineth therefore a day of rest for the people of God. For he that is entered into his rest, the same also hath rested from his works, as God did from his. Let us hasten therefore to enter into that rest; lest any man fall into the same example of unbelief. (Heb. 4:9-11)

The Psalms of David also remind us of the virtue of steadfastness, immovability—what we might call a holy stubbornness. "My persecutors will exult if ever I should be moved" (Ps. 12:5). But the faithful man says: "Ever will I keep the Lord before my eyes: for with Him at my right, I shall not be moved" (Ps. 15:8). Indeed, he begs the Lord: "Make firm my steps in Thy ways, that my footsteps not be moved" (Ps. 16:5). Our enemies, both spiritual and temporal, demonic and democratic, wish to shake us up or thrust us out of the narrow way of truth, but they will not succeed if the Lord Himself, who is an immovable Rock, strengthens our feet, that they not be moved.

THE GOD-MAN, OUR ULTIMATE ROCK

In the Holy Bible, God speaks to us with a variety of images, each of which conveys some aspect of the infinite truth that our finite minds can never fully comprehend. Of these images, one that has always been greatly cherished, not only for obvious architectural reasons, but also and primarily for its function as a spiritual metaphor, is that of the rock.

Scripture compares both Christ and His Church to a *rock*. Of all the natural materials we know in the world, rock is the most firm, the most solid. It can serve as the foundation for everything else because it is stable and unchangeable. Rock is found in massive deposits—in vast mountain ranges, canyons, the bottom of the sea, in fact everywhere on Earth. The earth seems to *be* primarily rock. Rocks are ancient. When all else is changing, they abide. This is why Scripture speaks of the "everlasting hills" (Gen. 49:26, Deut. 33:15, etc.) and "mount Sion," which, like the Lord Himself, "shall not be moved for ever" (Ps. 124:1).

According to Scripture, Jesus Christ Himself is the rock of the Church. He is the rock on which the wise man builds his house, so that the rain, floods, and winds cannot sweep it away (cf. Mt. 7:24–27). He is the living stone, rejected by men but chosen and made honorable by God, a chief cornerstone, elect, precious; and the one who believes in Him shall not be confounded (cf. 1 Pet. 2:4–8). He is the stone rejected by the builders, who has become the cornerstone (cf. Mt. 21:42; Eph. 2:19–20). He is a stumbling stone and a rock of scandal (cf. Rom. 9:33). He is the spiritual rock from which the children of Israel drink their fill (cf. 1 Cor. 10:4). The Epistle to the Hebrews throws down the gauntlet to the cult of change: "Jesus Christ is the same yesterday, today, and forever" (Heb. 13:8).[1] He is, so to speak, the Platonic form of rock—the living, intelligent, divine Rock that, unlike material rock, is truly beyond the clutches of time and change.

THE VICAR OF CHRIST AS ROCK

In the sixteenth chapter of St. Matthew's Gospel, Our Lord declares that Simon, too, shall be called a rock—the very meaning of the name "Peter."[2] St. Peter, as head of the apostles, is to exhibit the same properties as rock so that he may be the foundation the Church needs, especially whenever storms of heresy, schism, apostasy, tyrannical governments, laxity, and lukewarmness buffet the house. The pope is called the vicar of Christ not because he

---

1   See Kwasniewski, "Cult of Change," in *Ministers of Christ*, 235–46.
2   There is an obvious word play in the Greek: "You are *Petros*, and on this *petra* I will build my Church." Even Protestant commentators now widely recognize that Jesus is talking about Peter here, without negating the additional meanings the passage has.

substitutes for Christ, but because—to the extent possible on Earth, assisted by Heaven—he represents Him, shepherds His people, enforces His rights, and defends His interests. "Vicar of Christ" is no mere "historical title."[3]

After his great confession of the divinity of Christ, Peter is rewarded with these words: "Flesh and blood hath not revealed this to thee, but my Father who is in heaven. And I say to thee that thou art Rock, and upon this rock I will build my Church." What is this "flesh and blood" incapable of revealing divine mysteries to the soul? It is Peter's *humanity*, his human reasonings, his deductions based on sense data—even his "religious sense," however well developed it was. Flesh and blood are inherently changing, unstable, incapable of attaining the knowledge and love of God in Himself—and the same is true of intellectual fashions and schools of philosophy.

One might imagine Our Lord saying to Peter: "It is not Platonism or Aristotelianism, not idealism or rationalism or materialism or any other -ism that has revealed to you Who I am. My Father, sovereignly free, has revealed it by His gracious pleasure. You are the beneficiary of His light. This is how it will be in the Church that I am founding: what you must know about God and about the life and destiny of man has been and will be *shown* to you at the right time, and this precious gift you shall jealously guard and faithfully pass down, so that the same revealed truth may spread to every tribe and tongue and people and nation, until the end of time."

STRAYING FROM THE ARDUOUS PATHS

But as we know, Peter immediately falls from this lofty height by returning to the comfortable world of secular thought. When Jesus announces His imminent suffering and death, Peter accommodates himself to the mentality of a Jewish zealot: "God forbid, Lord! This shall never happen to you" (Mt. 16:22). Here, Peter shows the flesh and blood of which he is made, and what is worse, he attempts to force the eternal Son of God into the mold of this fallible flesh and blood. This is why he earns the Lord's sharp rebuke: "Get behind me, Satan! You are a hindrance to me; for you are not on the side of God, but of men" (Mt. 16:23). Or, as

3   See "Pope Francis drops 'Vicar of Christ' title in Vatican yearbook," *LifeSiteNews*, April 2, 2020.

another translation has it: "thou savourest not the things that are of God, but the things that are of men."[4]

It is no coincidence that Our Lord said something similar to Satan himself, in chapter 4 of the same Gospel: "Get thee hence, Satan: for it is written, Thou shalt worship the Lord thy God, and him only shalt thou serve" (Mt. 4:1). The word "Satan" means "adversary" or "opposer" or "plotter against,"[5] and the way he opposes the divine plan is to set up a false worship of himself or of those worldly goods that will lead their worshiper to hell. Secular accommodationism, the idea that we are to adapt ourselves to the world and adopt its pattern, is the most subtle form of Satanism (cf. Rom. 12:2). To this idolatry of the world and the flesh we may apply the words of St. Paul: "God gave them up in the lusts of their hearts to impurity, to the dishonoring of their bodies among themselves, because they exchanged the truth about God for a lie and worshiped and served the creature rather than the Creator, who is blessed for ever!" (Rom. 1:24-25).

In the period of the Fathers of the Church—happily free from both the anti-papal exegesis of later Protestant heretics *and* the "insane pope-centrism and papolatry"[6] of modern times—exegetes of Scripture did not hesitate to connect the "rock" of Matthew 16 with Christ Himself,[7] and with the virtue of faith that unites us to His truth. In the same vein, St. Thomas Aquinas comments: "But what is this? Are both Christ and Peter the foundation? One should say that Christ is the foundation through Himself, but Peter insofar as he holds the confession of Christ, insofar as he is His vicar."[8]

---

4   See Joseph Ratzinger, *Called to Communion: Understanding the Church Today*, trans. Adrian Walker (San Francisco: Ignatius Press, 1996), 60-61, 72-74. "Left to his own resources, the one who by God's grace is permitted to be the bedrock is a stone on the path that makes the foot stumble" (61).

5   Old English *Satan*, from Late Latin *Satan* (in Vulgate in Old Testament only), from Greek *Satanas*, from Hebrew *satan* "adversary, one who plots against another," from *satan* "to show enmity to, oppose, plot against," from the root *s-t-n* "one who opposes, obstructs, or acts as an adversary."

6   A phrase from Bishop Schneider in an interview from January 2018. See "Bishop Schneider Interview: Catholics must not 'become victims of an insane pope-centrism,'" *LifeSiteNews*, January 4, 2018.

7   St. Thomas: *"upon this rock,* i.e., upon you, Peter, because from me, the Rock, you receive that you are a rock. And just as I am a rock, so upon you, Peter, I will build my Church" (*Commentary on Matthew*, n. 1383).

8   Aquinas, *Commentary*, n. 1384.

FIDELITY TO THE ROCK OF UNCHANGING FAITH

Peter is a rock *by holding and publicly professing the faith of Christ and His Church*. In the "Pledge of fidelity to the authentic teaching of the Church by pro-life and pro-family leaders," published on the feast of Our Lady of Guadalupe, December 12, 2017, we find a perfect expression of this faith:

> We pledge our full obedience to the hierarchy of the Catholic Church in the legitimate exercise of its authority. However, nothing will ever persuade us, or compel us, to abandon or contradict any article of the Catholic faith or any truth definitively established. If there is any conflict between the words and acts of any member of the hierarchy, even the pope, and the doctrine that the Church has always taught, we will remain faithful to the perennial teaching of the Church. If we were to depart from the Catholic faith, we would depart from Jesus Christ, to whom we wish to be united for all eternity.[9]

---

9   Text at www.fidelitypledge.com.

8

Trials in the Church: Blessings in Disguise

T HE "INDEFECTIBILITY" OF THE CHURCH means that the hierarchy and the faithful, and thus, the sacramental and social life of the Church, will always remain intact *somewhere*. We know that it cannot mean *everywhere*, otherwise the fall of north Africa to the Moslems, or the schism of half of Europe during the Protestant revolt, would never have been possible. We know that it cannot be *nowhere*, as if the Church would disappear into an invisible ideal to be rediscovered later—as Protestants often believe happened to the Church from about AD 300 to 1500.

The reason so many people are renewing their study of the Arian crisis is that there were indeed times during that terrible trial when very few bishops and priests were really Catholic, as compared with a vast number on the heretical side. Athanasius made a famous quip, "You have the buildings but we have the faith," because most of the physical churches were in the hands of Arians or semi-Arians.

On February 22 each year, the Church celebrates the feast of the Chair of St. Peter, when we recall Our Lord's bestowal of the keys of the kingdom on the Prince of the Apostles and the establishment of the latter's episcopal seat in the city of Rome. It is a salutary annual reminder to us both that the Church is founded on the rock of St. Peter, a visible head, *and* that the essence of this rock is Peter's faith in the Divine Redeemer, whose Passion for the sake of the truth He must make His own, in order to be worthy of the great office conferred on him, and to execute its responsibilities well.

Matthew 16:18—"thou art Peter, and upon this rock I will build my church, and the gates of hell shall not prevail against it"—has a long exegetical history. St. Augustine took "rock" to mean the faith of Peter and therefore the faith of the Church. St. Thomas Aquinas argued that it referred both to Peter's act of faith, which every Christian can emulate, and to Peter's position of authority, which he alone receives.

In the Counter-Reformation period, the application of Matthew 16:18 to the papacy was obviously foremost in the Catholic mind, but the whole context of Matthew 16 shows that what Jesus is praising is Peter's confession of faith in His divinity and messianic mission; *this* is the foundation of the Church, not a man or even an office, abstractly considered. The fundamental duty of the pope is to continue to confess Christ the Son of God by upholding the true Faith in all of its dogmatic and moral teachings—in other words, to ensure that the Gospel remains intact, undiluted, uncorrupted, unhidden. This already begins to tell us much about what's problematic with the current successor of St. Peter.

When someone recently challenged me "You need to adjust your critique based on a wider view of Church history. I mean, look at Alexander VI!," I replied: "Having studied papal history, I would take Alexander VI in a heartbeat. Whatever his moral failings, in his official capacity he upheld the teaching of the Church and humbly submitted to the venerable liturgical rites of Rome. He did the minimum that a pope is required to do—he kept traditional doctrine and worship intact."

Yes, Matthew 16:18 (with surrounding verses) is definitely talking about a person and *his* faith, which is the basis for the gift of a special role from Christ; but the key to the role being properly lived is the possession and exercise of the very same faith. A heretical or apostate pope would be a contradiction in terms; indeed, he would cancel himself out, like +2 and –2 in algebra. Of course, we know that this heresy or apostasy would have to be manifest, called out as such, and stubbornly maintained in the face of challenge.

Given the hardships of the moment, I am not surprised that a reader wrote to me:

> Why does God "help" us to a certain point, but not more? For example, why would God not allow His Church to fail, but then let her get close anyway—why not draw the line sooner? Or in Genesis, why allow Adam the freedom to choose to eat from the tree of knowledge of good and evil, but then prevent him the chance to eat from the tree of life—why not protect him more from the first tree? Of course, with no help from God we would be hopelessly lost; but how can we grasp just "how much"

He chooses to help us? In a way, it can almost seem like it's a "game" to God; but I have to assume there is some divine order to it.

This is the question of all questions. Why does God permit evil at all? Why does He permit this much and not more—or less? I see the answer in terms of the "severe mercy" that Sheldon Vanauken talks about. God is not trying to make it easy for us; He aims to sanctify us, ween us from sin, and make heroes of us. Every Christian is called to be a martyr, whether bloody or unbloody. His mercy is demanding, and it will take us to the very edge, the limit. When we embrace this, we do our purgatory on earth, so to speak. That is the teaching of the mystics, too, such as St. John of the Cross: the purgative way, the illuminative way, and the unitive way. If we want union with our Lord, we must let Him teach us; and if we want to become teachable, ready to receive what He desires to give, we must suffer. Suffering stretches the capacity of our faith, our hope, and our charity.

God being infinite has so much to give that He must carve out the space for Himself in our souls through mighty trials and tribulations. Such is the essence of a love that will not and cannot compromise, that refuses to share space with any unworthy love.

I say this regarding the interior life of each Catholic, and each believer's vocation to witness to the truth, which is the essence of martyrdom. But there is also a benefit to the Church at large whenever God permits trials of this magnitude, namely, that the truth of her traditional teaching will shine all the more brightly when its enemies have been confounded. Our understanding of the papacy, its inseparable link with tradition, and the outer limits of its deviation will be deepened; our faith will be purified of hyperpapalism and sedevacantism.

IT HAS BEEN OBJECTED THAT CHRISTIANITY MAKES the refutation of itself impossible by claiming both that the gates of hell will not prevail and that false shepherds will come. So, whether things are going well or badly, either way the Church wins. Is this a logical problem? Should Christianity be "falsifiable" as other hypotheses are?

From the beginning, Christianity has offered a multi-faceted view of how the Church will fare over the ages. Neither *x* alone nor not-*x* alone is the evidence for Christianity's truth, but the presence of both over time, and indeed from the start of the Church to the end of time. If they weren't both present, then Matthew's Gospel, which most clearly makes the double claim, would be seen to be wrong.

But I think there is an important point we have to reflect on, and that is the need to shuffle off expectations based on historical contingencies and not on the nature of things. Let me explain.

There was a period in the Church beginning sometime after the post-Tridentine renewal (Counter-Reformation) and lasting up to the eve of Vatican II when we could truthfully say the Church flourished in terms of discipline, in terms of doctrine, and even in terms of money, and the (relative) lack of turbulence in the Church—at least as far as most pewsitters were concerned—was in fact a motivator for many to join it. "Look at this immensely powerful, stable, prestigious, coherent organization! It must be true!" This was the period people characterize as "triumphalist," and in a way they are right: The Church's worldly successes went to the heads of her leaders and made them feel that they, like Jesus, had done all things well.

Yet consider the danger. To the degree that members of the Church leaned too much on her successes as evidence of her divine identity and mission, to that degree her human failures—which have *always* been possible, and which past ages were quite full of—will *now* feel more like evidence against her claims.

One can still give an account of how none of this amounts to contradictions in teaching and how it still fits within the parameters of damage the Holy Spirit will allow to happen in the Church on earth. I do not think that just any Catholic's account would necessarily survive just any kind of new facts; that is, it would be falsifiable, and therefore not vulnerable to the charge that one has removed oneself from verifiability. For example, if someone in the first millennium would have claimed that a pope will always be present in the city of Rome, his claim would have been falsified by the Avignon period, when popes lived in France; and if someone in the twentieth century had claimed that a pope could never teach error in any way, that claim would have been falsified *at least* by the pontificate of Pope Francis, as is evident to anyone who reads the book *Defending the Faith Against Present Heresies.*

Of course, making a defense of the Church's indefectibility, especially today, takes knowledge, time, and patience. It is not something that can be done in a social media exchange. That leaves the scandalous problem: What about people on the outside who do not have a sufficient reason or motivation to listen to a long and careful account of how to reconcile things that sure *look* contradictory? If the Church turns people away from the path to heaven by her chaotic external appearances, have not the gates of hell prevailed?

But this objection is really no different from the generic problem of scandal. Every scandal that results from the abuse of human freedom is, by definition, the placing of an obstacle to the truth. Scandal is, well, scandalous: it makes it possible for certain people to fail to reach something good or true because of some evil or error that trips them up along the way. But the existence of scandals is not, by its nature, incompatible with the Spirit's guidance of the Church as a whole over time, nor with entering and maintaining a grace-filled relationship with Christ here and now.

A friend of mine recently spoke with a young man who entered the Church a year and a half ago, and the story of his journey was astounding. He told of friends on Twitter (of all places) who got him to start thinking about Catholicism; he told about a priest who urged him *not* to enter the Church but to "live out his vocation" in his Protestant community (!); he told about an SSPX priest who gave him solid answers and did not pressure him to join the SSPX. The path he followed was by no means an *obvious* path. Yet he and others continue to enter the Church, despite how impossible it feels to all of us who are so close to the scandals.

The possibility and the probability and the actuality of scandal confronts me with an existential question: What is the Church, what is Catholicism, who is Christ, for me? Can I perceive and hold on to what is true, what is good, and what is beautiful in the midst of smokescreens, counterfeits, hideous distortions? Isn't the fact that I can recognize and lament what is not true, not good, or not beautiful a kind of proof that the Lord's voice is not silenced by the noise and the dissonance?

It is a cause of real hope that more Catholics than ever—thanks, ironically, to the internet—are questioning the "great reset" of Catholicism at and after the Second Vatican Council and rediscovering traditional Catholic doctrine and liturgy and *life*. Yes, we *can* try to live our lives as the saints did, as prior generations of Catholics tried to do at their best. What is to prevent us? Some abusers and corrupters in Rome? Really? Or is it our own fear of looking silly or being embarrassed when we refrain from meat on Fridays, pray the daily Rosary, go out of our way to attend the traditional Latin Mass, dress modestly in the summer, avoid offensive films and books? There is no need whatsoever to be ashamed of any of these things; on the contrary, the more the modernists undermine the Catholic religion as it has always been taught, the more powerful and crucial is our witness—and, I would even say, the more sanctifying for us who must bear many crosses our ancestors could not have dreamed of, but which God always knew would come.

When Christ established His Church with miracles and clear teaching and built it on the rock of Peter, the most obvious conclusion at the time would have been: "Fantastic! At last a religion that cannot be corrupted!" That's what we'd all have expected. And this is why Christ, to our surprise, tells us: "Ah yes, but there will be goats mixed in with the sheep, and wolves entering the fold as well; there will be false prophets who will almost deceive the elect. You can recognize them by their fruits—and you know that I have told you ahead of time." This, to me, is not "convenient" (as the skeptic might say), but rather, prophetic, strengthening, and comforting. I know that the sky is not falling in on the Catholic Church, the Mystical Body of Christ; instead, alas, it is temporarily ransacked by perverts and heretics. They cannot alter one iota of the deposit of faith or change the testimony of the ages—of the saints, the great councils, the crystal clear teaching of umpteen catechisms.[1] Even if they take away access to the sacraments, they cannot take away our faith or the grace of God. These do not belong to them.

The drunken sailors of the ship are doing their best to run it aground or sink it, but the ship sails on. It sails by a power inherent in it, not by the muscle of the oarsmen. They could abolish the

---

1   See the Tradivox project.

Creed but it would remain true; they can modify sacramental rites past recognition but they cannot abolish sacraments in their traditional form, which will always survive somewhere; they can throw up obstacles to grace but they cannot prevent God from giving His grace to souls who desire it and ask for it; they can modify the Lord's Prayer in Italian or any other language, but what the Greek New Testament actually says remains unchanged. It's still possible to be a Catholic in spite of everything; it is always worthwhile to be a Catholic, because the Catholic Faith is true, good, beautiful, and salvific. That is all it needs to be for us to love it and cleave to it.

9
Does Pius VI's *Auctorem Fidei* Support Paul VI's Novus Ordo?

ALTHOUGH THIS BOOK DOES NOT ENTER extensively into liturgical questions, it will nonetheless be extremely useful at this juncture, in pursuing our main theme of the nature and limits of the papacy, to examine an objection brought against critics of the Novus Ordo by its more sophisticated defenders, who believe they must accept and enforce this novelty in order to uphold papal authority. These defenders will cite various magisterial documents of the past—above all, Pope Pius VI's *Auctorem Fidei* n. 78 and Pope Gregory XVI's regional letter *Quo Graviora* n. 10—as definitive proofs that the pope (and therefore the Church on behalf of which he acts) cannot promulgate defective, useless, or harmful liturgical rites. Those who wield these texts do not realize, however, the trap into which they are falling.

Let us consider more closely what Pius VI condemned. The Italian regional Synod of Pistoia (1786), under the influence of Jansenism and Enlightenment rationalism, had argued that in the realm of Church discipline,

> there is to be distinguished what is necessary or useful to retain the faithful in spirit, from that which is useless or too burdensome for the liberty of the sons of the New Covenant to endure, but more so, from that which is dangerous or harmful, namely, leading to superstition and materialism.

Note that this position enjoyed a second and more vigorous life among the liturgical reformers of the 1960s, who separated "what is necessary or useful to retain" from "that which is useless or too burdensome" (e.g., the fasting and abstinence enjoined by the missal prayers in Lent[1]) and who waged an implacable campaign against things in the old liturgy they found "dangerous or harmful," such as praying for the conversion of the Jews, proclaiming no

---

1   See Yves Daoudal, "Non Possumus," *Rorate Caeli*, February 1, 2022.

salvation outside the Church, accepting the damnation of Judas and the threat of hell for the rest of us, putting forward the so-called legendary saints and their legendary miracles, manifesting a "preoccupation" with sin and an excessive emphasis on the world to come, encouraging the veneration of relics, and so forth.[2] At the Synod of Pistoia itself, the program of reform included a simplification of rites, use of the vernacular, abolition of silent priestly prayers, and a removal of side altars.

Pius VI goes on to condemn the Pistoians, saying that their opinion

> includes and submits to a prescribed examination even the discipline established and approved by the Church, as if the Church which is ruled by the Spirit of God could have established discipline which is not only useless and burdensome for Christian liberty to endure, but which is even dangerous and harmful and leading to superstition and materialism,—false, rash, scandalous, dangerous, offensive to pious ears, injurious to the Church and to the Spirit of God by whom it is guided, at least erroneous.

In this utterance he is condemning in advance the reform of Bugnini, the Consilium, and Montini, which agree closely with the platform of Pistoia.[3] It would therefore be entirely illogical and self-contradictory to attempt to apply *Auctorem Fidei* of the year 1794, when the liturgy Pius VI was defending was none other than the Tridentine rite, to the Novus Ordo of 1969, which Paul VI intended as a replacement for the imperfect and no longer profitable rite of Pius V. Pius VI is appealing to the objective truth that the Church cannot err in approving her traditional liturgy; therefore in approving a non-traditional liturgy that departs from the uninterrupted chain of ecclesial transmission, it is Paul VI who runs afoul of his predecessor's condemnation, not (e.g.) Archbishop Lefebvre.

---

2   Some of these problems already appeared in liturgical reforms prior to the 1960s, but they did not dominate until the work of the Consilium under Msgr. Bugnini.

3   In his revealing book *The Synod of Pistoia and Vatican II: Jansenism and the Struggle for Catholic Reform* (New York: Oxford University Press, 2019), Shaun Blanchard candidly acknowledges (and celebrates) the parallels between that condemned council and Vatican II, including in the area of liturgical reform.

In Gregory XVI's *Quo Graviora*, we see the same dynamic at work.[4] Written in 1833, not even forty years after *Auctorem Fidei*, the text makes it immediately clear that the pope is responding to the German cousins of the Pistoian heretics, whom he sees as moved by a "wicked passion for introducing novelties into the Church." He describes their views:

> They state categorically that there are many things in the discipline of the Church in the present day, in its government, and in the form of its external worship which are not suited to the character of our time. These things, they say, should be changed, as they are harmful for the growth and prosperity of the Catholic religion, before the teaching of faith and morals suffers any harm from it. Therefore, showing a zeal for religion and showing themselves as an example of piety, they force reforms, conceive of changes, and pretend to renew the Church.

Sounds strangely familiar, doesn't it? This is precisely the rhetoric used by the central and northern European faction at the Second Vatican Council, as we find it carefully documented in Roberto de Mattei's work (completing the documentation done by Ralph Wiltgen in *The Rhine Flows into the Tiber*).[5]

Continues Gregory: "They contend that the entire exterior form of the Church can be changed indiscriminately" and "the present discipline of the Church rests on failures, obscurities, and other inconveniences of this kind." These sentiments, voiced relentlessly around the time of the last ecumenical Council, shaped the implementation of it, especially in the area of the sacred liturgy. "They attack this Holy See as if it were too persistent in outdated customs and did not look deeply inside the character of our time"—this was said in 1833, but it might as well have been 1963!

> They accuse this See of becoming blind amid the light of new knowledge, and of hardly distinguishing those things

---

4   This encyclical should not be confused with the better-known *Quo Graviora* of 1826, one of many papal encyclicals condemning Freemasonry.
5   See de Mattei, *Second Vatican Council*. It would seem that few of the advocates of "ressourcement" who loudly defend Vatican II have bothered to study this painstakingly researched account by a master historian who demonstrates the domination of progressivist theology at the council.

which deal with the substance of religion from those which regard only the external form. They say that it feeds superstition, fosters abuses, and finally behaves as if it never looks after the interests of the Catholic Church in changing times.... Nor do We want to discuss their errors concerning the new *Rituale* written in the vernacular, which they want to have adapted more to the character of our times.

It's both comical and tragic to see the parallels between the rebelliousness Gregory is condemning and the progressivist attitudes that prevailed at Vatican II, encouraged and rewarded by a sympathetic Paul VI. Yes, he was not *as* progressivist as some others were, and on certain issues he was capable of reaffirming traditional doctrine; nevertheless, the same can be said of the Pistoians and the Germans, who leaned Catholic on some points and Jansenist/Protestant on others.

Now we come to the important paragraph 10, in which I will highlight the lines that are lifted out of context and thrown in the faces of traditionalists:

These men [i.e., the self-styled reformers] want to utterly reform the holy institution of sacramental penance. They insolently slander the Church and falsely accuse it of error, and their shamelessness should be deplored even more. They claim that the Church, by ordering annual confession, allowing indulgences as an added condition of fulfilling confession, and permitting private Eucharist and daily works of piety, has weakened that salutary tradition[6] and subtracted from its power and efficacy. *The*

---

6   As you might have guessed, the Pistoians and their German cousins held the error of antiquarianism: like the twentieth-century liturgical reformers, they maintained that the liturgy of the Church had become corrupt and needed to be freed of its "accretions" and "restored" to a "more authentic" earlier form, which they curiously fashioned largely out of their own heads, as the Protestants had done before them, and with contempt for known elements of early liturgy that had survived in the traditional rites. This is why Pius XII made the same connection I am making when he warned that the liturgical movement right before Vatican II had been to some extent compromised by "the exaggerated and senseless antiquarianism to which the illegal Council of Pistoia gave rise" (*Mediator Dei*, 64). See "The Problem of False Antiquarianism" in Peter Kwasniewski, *Reclaiming Our Roman Catholic Birthright* (Brooklyn, NY: Angelico Press, 2020), 149–60.

Church is the pillar and foundation of truth—all of which truth is taught by the Holy Spirit. Should the Church be able to order, yield to, or permit those things which tend toward the destruction of souls and the disgrace and detriment of the sacrament instituted by Christ? Those proponents of new ideas who are eager to foster true piety in the people should consider that, with the frequency of the sacraments diminished or entirely eliminated, religion slowly languishes and finally perishes.

As teachers remind their students again and again, context makes all the difference. Gregory defends the Church's inability to go astray in the directing of the sacraments *because* the Church, as the pillar and foundation of truth, has *always* taught and acted consistently in regard to them. In other words, as with Pius VI, Gregory cannot conceive of a good Catholic who would "utterly reform" anything and thereby commit insolent slander against the Church by holding her to have erred in her long-standing discipline. Paul VI, on the contrary, held that the liturgy's being in Latin was an *obstacle* to the salvation of souls: for him, this 1,600-year-old custom redounded to the "disgrace and detriment" of the sacraments.[7]

The sharpest irony is that the sacrament that was hit the hardest and suffered the most catastrophic decline in the Church after Vatican II was none other than the "holy institution of sacramental penance." The German radicals condemned by Gregory wanted to make penance more "meaningful" by freeing it from routine and obligation, something you did when and as you needed it; and Gregory predicted that the resulting decrease in confessions would eventually cause religion to languish and perish. That's what comes of "proponents of new ideas who are eager to foster true piety in the people"—or, at any rate, what *they* think of as "true piety." How many ideas in the 1960s were advanced under the banner of "freedom" and "maturity" and "a personal living faith" and so on? And how many millions of the faithful, with their new-found freedom and their assumption of worldly maturity, began to fall away? Without the institutional pattern and pressure they had no bearings any more, no support.

---

7   See "A Half-Century of Novelty: Revisiting Paul VI's Apologia for the New Mass," *Rorate Caeli*, April 2, 2019.

In short: Gregory XVI might as well be describing the liturgical and sacramental fallout of Vatican II, stemming from the same kind of false principles as the ones he diagnosed and condemned among certain Germans of his day. The same can be said of Pius VI with regard to the Italians of *his* day a few decades earlier. These popes are defending as the work of God and the rock-solid witness of the Church all the *traditional liturgical rites* that the would-be reformers of the Enlightenment era criticize as faulty and arrogantly propose to recast or renew. Either these popes are correct about the traditional rites of the Church, and the twentieth-century reformers are no better than their Pistoian and German forerunners; or the entire rationale of *Auctorem Fidei* and *Quo Graviora* falls apart. You can't have it both ways.

Now I fully admit that Gregory XVI in *Quo Graviora* strongly reasserts the sole prerogative of the pope to make determinations about liturgy and sacraments. In the Tridentine perspective, wherein the Church must gather her children tightly together against errors and depredations from without, it makes sense that such grave decisions would be reserved to the Holy See, even if for much of Church history they were not. However, as before, Gregory asserts this authority because he sees the pope's role as *protecting and passing on what the Church already believes and does*—not because he wants to turn things upside-down as the radicals wish to do. Put simply, the popes are not relativists who think anything goes as long as a pope signs off on it, or nominalists who think that if a pope says white is black, it's black; nor are they voluntarists who think that if he declares X to be good, even if it's bad, it will suddenly become good, or vice versa.

As someone online once put it: "The pope does not have the ontological power to decree tradition not-really-tradition, to decree an innovation more-or-less-tradition, to decree a destruction and invention a reform, or to decree an open, proclaimed, and lauded discontinuity a secret continuity. He can do things by force but he can't make them *not* be what they *are*." I'm with Aquinas on this one (against Ockham): not even God has the power to change the past or to violate the principle of non-contradiction.

God indeed protects the Church from promulgating invalid sacramental rites—no serious theologian questions the bare validity of the Novus Ordo. But as Ratzinger himself noted again and again, the fashioning of the Novus Ordo replaced organic development with "the model of technical production" stemming from ideas already condemned.[8] That is why he could say that the suppression of the Latin Mass "introduced a breach into the history of the liturgy whose consequences could only be tragic."[9] These foreseen tragic consequences were the very reason Pius VI and Gregory XVI condemned what they did.

So the next time someone cites these papal documents or others like them against the traditionalist view, thinking he's just won the debate, you may reply with a twinkle: "No, on the contrary, they support our view, and they undermine yours. What else would you expect from popes who wrote 175 years and 136 years prior to the advent of the New Mass? And if they had been granted a prophetic vision of it, you can be sure they'd have condemned *its* architects a hundred times more fiercely than they did the presumptuous reformers of their day."

---

8   Johannes Bökmann, "Liturgiereform: Nicht Wiederbelebung sondern Verwüstung," *Theologisches* 20.2 (February 1990): 103-4, quoting Ratzinger's contribution to the book *Simandron—Der Wachklopfer. Gedenkschrift für Klaus Gamber (1919–1989)*.

9   Joseph Ratzinger, *Milestones*, trans. Erasmo Leiva-Merikakis (San Francisco, CA: Ignatius Press, 1998), 146-48.

10

Are Traditionalists Guilty of "Private Judgment" Over the Popes?

R OD DREHER AT THE AMERICAN CONSER-
vative *mentioned a friend of his who had compared me to Luther.
This provocation deserved a response, which I sent to Mr. Dreher,
and which he added as Update #6 to his post "Pope Francis, Ever the Icon-
oclast" of December 18, 2021.*

DEAR ROD,

I appreciated that you quoted my article in your December 18th post. There is of course much in your writing (in general) that I can agree with, or at the very least sympathize with. Nevertheless, I was surprised when a correspondent of yours compared me with Luther (presumably in the sense that Protestants set themselves up as little popes who determine what's true and false by some kind of private judgment or idiosyncratic reading of the Christian tradition), and I hope you will allow me the opportunity to make a brief response. I cannot claim to be speaking for all Catholic traditionalists but I suspect most would agree with what follows.

I find it frankly astonishing that anyone would confuse the traditionalist position with Luther's. Luther quickly moved from opposing papal vices to opposing the papacy as such, then a bunch of ecumenical councils, then many Fathers and Doctors of the Church. He called reason a whore, and heaped contempt on the scholastics, especially St. Thomas Aquinas—rather different from the habits of a trained Thomist who follows the master's principles, makes frequent use of his reasoning, and looks to his life as exemplary. [1]

---

1   See, e.g., my books *The Ecstasy of Love in the Thought of Thomas Aquinas* (Steubenville, OH: Emmaus Academic, 2021) and *True Obedience in the Church* (Manchester, NH: Sophia Institute Press, 2021), and my article "A Mystic Who Shed Tears During Mass: Revising Our Image of St. Thomas Aquinas," *New Liturgical Movement*, March 6, 2020.

Traditional Catholics can point to literally hundreds of catechisms published with papal or episcopal approval over the centuries that all teach exactly the same faith. They can point to extant liturgical books from every century and see the same Roman rite in various stages of its career, but always recognizably the same family—a family from which the Novus Ordo is excluded by every criterion. They can point to consistent teaching on all major matters of faith and morals from the popes of every century.

To base one's faith on such a mighty witness of *objective Catholicism*, treasuring the unity of faith and reason, is the very opposite of the nominalism, voluntarism, and subjectivism of Luther and the religious pluralism to which it necessarily leads. Remember, the ones who are praising Luther and toying with his ideas are the progressives led by Francis. The campaign against the historic worship of the Latin-rite Church is nominalist and voluntarist to the core. For Bugnini and Montini, and now for Bergoglio and Roche, the Roman Rite is whatever the authorities say it is, regardless of reality (e.g., as Matthew Hazell proves, only 13% of the euchology of the traditional rite survived unchanged in the new one). [2] If we *want* the liturgical reform to have been necessary and successful, then it *was* and *is* necessary and successful, with no statistics or experiences to the contrary counting for anything. All this is a parody of the rational faith to which Catholics adhere in their traditional doctrine and practice, inherited and passed on with utmost respect.

The unified witness of Roman Catholicism does not run into serious difficulties until the popes of and after the Second Vatican Council. And even these popes vary a great deal in the kind of problems they present to us: each is a mixed bag, at times a very large bag of very mixed content. Paul VI gave us *Humanae Vitae* and a ruptured, ersatz liturgy; John Paul II gave us *Veritatis Splendor* and the Assisi interreligious gatherings; Benedict XVI gave us *Summorum Pontificum* and a miserable abdication. Francis, nevertheless, is the outsized modernist who is slashing and burning much of what his predecessors revered, actions which are not

---

2   See Matthew Hazell, "'All the Elements of the Roman Rite'? Mythbusting, Part II," *New Liturgical Movement*, October 1, 2021. Mr. Hazell's more detailed research, for which he supplies all the documentation, corrects the older figure of 17% proposed by Fr. Anthony Cekada.

and cannot be called Catholic by any stretch of the imagination.

Take two examples: the death penalty (about which I gave a lecture in Chicago[3]) and communion for those living in an objective state of adultery (concerning which I was involved in a number of public statements).[4] If Pope Francis is right, then all of his predecessors are wrong—and so, for that matter, are the Old and New Testaments, as interpreted by the Fathers and Doctors. But if all that is *right*, then Pope Francis is, quite simply, wrong. Now, which is easier to believe possible? Which of the alternatives is less destructive to the Catholic Faith? In fact, the former position destroys it altogether, while the latter only shatters an exaggerated ultramontanism extrapolated from but not necessitated by Vatican I.[5]

Yes, some of the modern popes have let the "spirit of Vatican I" go to their heads and speak as if they are the Delphic oracles of the Church, but this is a far cry from what Catholics are obliged to believe by what is definitively taught in the extraordinary Magisterium or the universal ordinary Magisterium. It is commonplace to point out, for instance, that not everything in an encyclical is taught with equal authority and that errors are indeed *possible*. No less possible would be an erroneous manner of speaking or a faulty trend of thinking that does not compromise the faith and morals of the Church as such. Theologians have long distinguished between primary and secondary elements in papal documents, and between the essential content asserted and the accidents with which it is surrounded. If this leaves us sometimes in a muddle or a quandary, what's the big deal? The history of theology, whether in the East or in the West, has been rather messy—I say this just in case it might have escaped someone's attention. For a Catholic, the fundamental points of the Faith are luminously clear and nothing a pope can say or do will shake them. At least, that is what a traditional Catholic thinks. The progressives and modernists call such a one a "fundamentalist."

Those who would be tempted to say in response to the last paragraph: "Then what *good* is the papacy?" have evidently not spent much time studying history to see the countless, often crucial

---

3   See volume 2, chapter 40.
4   See Lamont and Pierantoni, *Defending the Faith*.
5   See Pauper Peregrinus, "Papal Infallibility."

ways in which one or another of the 266 successors of Peter have intervened when no one else could or would, in order to clarify or reaffirm Catholic truth when it was under attack, or to resolve an intractable administrative dilemma. The glories that can be attributed to a pivotal office that has endured for twenty centuries are not canceled out because of moments of shame and chaos.

Returning to our point of departure: for a Catholic to question and reject what Francis is doing is therefore nothing at all like Luther or Lutheranism. On the contrary, it has been Francis and his progressive allies who keep *praising* Luther, going so far as to put out a statue of him at the Vatican, and placing him, with Melanchthon, on one of their official stamps.[6] It was the Catholic liturgical reformers who imitated Luther by creating a new liturgy from the bits and pieces they still agreed with from the old one plus lots of novelties, holding that they must overcome a thousand years of corruption.[7] The parallels with Cranmer in England are even more striking.[8]

I have written much on these topics; those who are interested might wish to read "My Journey from Ultramontanism to Catholicism"[9]; "Beyond 'Smells and Bells': Why We Need the Objective Content of the *Usus Antiquior*"[10]; "The Pope's Boundedness to Tradition as a Legislative Limit: Replying to Ultramontanist Apologetics"[11]; and *True Obedience in the Church: A Guide to Discernment in Challenging Times.*[12]

I wish you and all your readers many graces this Christmas.

Peter Kwasniewski

---

6   See John-Henry Westen, "A statue of Luther in the Vatican and a new papal definition of 'lukewarm,'" *LifeSiteNews*, October 25, 2016; Crux Staff, "Vatican issues stamp featuring Martin Luther for Reformation anniversary," *Crux*, November 26, 2017.

7   See "Surprising Convergences between an Anti-Catholic Textbook and the Liturgical Reform," *New Liturgical Movement*, August 5, 2019.

8   See "Charting Liturgical Change" (www.whispersofrestoration.com/chart) and "New and Traditional side-by-side" (https://lms.org.uk/missals).

9   See chapter 1.

10   *Rorate Caeli*, November 29, 2019.

11   In Peter A. Kwasniewski, ed., *From Benedict's Peace to Francis's War: Catholics Respond to the Motu Proprio* Traditionis Custodes *on the Latin Mass* (Brooklyn, NY: Angelico Press, 2021), 222–47.

12   Manchester, NH: Sophia Institute Press, 2021.

Selective Papal Adulation

T ODAY[1] IN THE UNITED STATES OF AMER-
ica, it is, of course, Independence Day. But in many parts
of the Catholic world, today was also (and in some places,
still is) the Commemoration of All Holy Popes, a day on which
to offer Mass in honor of the impressive band of saintly pontiffs, especially those who do not have a feastday of their own. It
therefore gives us an opportunity to reflect on the phenomenon
of those who fail to honor the dignity of the papal office and its
saintly incumbents because they have a skewed vision of what the
papacy is all about.

Today there are cardinals who tell us that the Holy Spirit is
speaking through Francis. But what, one might ask, were the same
prelates doing while Benedict was pope—were they following the
voice of the Holy Spirit speaking through Benedict? Were they
rushing to the defense of *Summorum Pontificum*—the papal letter
acknowledging the freedom of priests to offer the Traditional
Latin Mass—as they now rush to the defense of *Amoris Laetitia*?
Or was Ratzinger somehow "beyond the pale of polite society,"
whereas Bergoglio is a new and definitive spokesperson of mercy?
Perhaps the cardinals of the new paradigm have a secret instinct
by which they recognize which popes are mouthpieces of the
Spirit and which ones are not.

In reality, we are seeing here an obvious case of a double
standard. If the pope is progressive, he is the oracle of God. If
he is traditional, he is a stick in the mud, a carryover, a relic of
the past, regressive, nostalgic, hard-hearted, rigid, on the wrong
side of history. In this way, a personal agenda is allowed to serve
as the actual magisterium, or the magisterial filter that strains the
gnat of *Summorum* but swallows the camel of *Amoris*.

Some have accused traditional Catholics of a similar double
standard. They say we do the same thing: we exalt Benedict and
hold Francis at arm's length. But this is not true. A traditional

---

1   This article was published on July 4, 2018.

Catholic avoids the dilemma altogether because he is not an ultramontanist to begin with, who thinks that popes should be blindly followed in whatever they say. His allegiance is first and always to Sacred Scripture, Sacred Tradition, and the clearly and solemnly articulated Magisterium of all the centuries. He knows that these and these alone are the things permanently binding on every member of Christ's faithful, including—and perhaps especially—the pope.

Thus, it is no inconsistency for a traditionalist to say: "Benedict XVI was a better pope than Francis," because his reasoning is: "Benedict followed more closely the teachings and traditions handed down from the past, whereas Francis departs from them in many and notable ways." It is not at all about pitting one pope against the next, but rather, about seeing all the popes as defenders of the deposit of faith and servants of the servants of God.

Then there is the phenomenon of "selective adulation" in the practical realm. The same people who clamored for the washing of women's feet, which they finally got (if only for the Novus Ordo), would never dream of emulating Pope Francis's use of the so-called Benedictine altar arrangement, that is, the six (or seven) candlesticks and crucifix that surmount the papal altar. Their devotion even to the Great Leader has arbitrary limits. A progressive will follow the progressivism of the pope but not his occasional traditional examples. By so doing, they once again show their hand.

Many have said in recent years that the Church is facing another crisis like that of Arianism in the fourth century, only ours is much worse because, in its modernist inspiration, it undermines the very notion of dogma and the very essence of revealed religion.

A colleague of mine once said that our crisis today is *not* like that of Arianism because we are not dealing with an obvious denial of doctrine, but with squishy ambiguities and tergiversations. But I am not convinced that this is true, since there are binary questions that face us and that we cannot avoid answering. One answer proves a man a Catholic, the other shows him an unbeliever.

1. Do you accept doctrinal continuity or not—that is, do you think it matters whether or not contemporary papal and episcopal teaching conforms to that which, in the past, was laid down authoritatively as always and everywhere true?

2. Do you hold there are exceptionless moral rights and wrongs, that is, things that must always be done, and things that must always be avoided, regardless of any and every circumstance? Do you hold that there are precepts we must obey in order to be saved? Is there any good that would justify the committing of some evil, or would make it not evil? Can one ever sin for the sake of a greater good?

3. Is the pope the guardian of Catholic tradition, or its master and lord?

Each of these questions allows only a yes or no answer. Some in the Church answer one way, some answer the other way. This divides them as much as the divinity of Christ divided the Catholics from the Arians. And there are plenty who are sitting on the fence, trying not to ask or answer such questions, just as there were equivocators and temporizers in the fourth century. But anyone who refuses to answer rightly a question about faith or morals to which the right answer is already known will meet a condemnation little different from that of a staunch defender of the wrong answer.

I 2

"But the Pope Said So!": Failed Excuses on Judgment Day

PEOPLE OFTEN FIND IT DIFFICULT TO JUDGE about contemporary problems because current affairs are too "close" to us to be able to see them clearly. We feel too much immersed in them, almost as if we are treading water and trying not to drown. One useful way of gaining perspective is to step back in time, into *other* periods of crisis, and to speculate on what the implications of those crises might have been for Catholics living through them. Here, this exploration will take the form of hypothetical dialogues between Christ and a soul at its particular judgment.

SCENARIO #I TAKES PLACE IN THE YEAR 366.

The Judge: O Christian soul, why did you dare to sing the songs of the Arians, with their refrain "there was a time when He was not"? For in truth, there is no time when I was not. I am the eternal Son of the eternal Father.

Soul: Well... I was confused when Pope Liberius signed an accord with the Emperor. Everyone was saying that the pope had admitted that there could be some debate, you know, some flexibility in the formulas... that it was not all black-and-white...

The Judge: You should have known better. My Church has always confessed My divinity. When Arius arose, he was immediately condemned as a heretic. The truth was solemnly defined at the Council of Nicaea, and My saints have defended it ever since.

Soul: Who was I to judge? Hearing conflicting things, I figured: "If the pope is confused, then how could I be expected to know for sure?" Aren't we just supposed to follow the pope?

The Judge: You say: "Who was I to judge?" Yet in your baptism and chrismation I gave you the Spirit of Truth by which to distinguish truth from falsehood, and the duty of knowing your faith and following it unto death.

Soul: But what of the pope, the rock on which the Church is built?

98

The Judge: The papacy I established as a guardian of the unchanging truths of the Faith and a barrier against novelty. That is why he is called a rock and not sand. This Liberius, My thirty-sixth pope, was unworthy of his charge; he wavered when he should have stood firm. Seeing all time before me, I declare to you that he will be the only pope among the fifty-four bishops of Rome from St. Peter to St. Gelasius who will not be revered as a saint.

Soul: I am ashamed. I stand justly condemned for my failure in faith. Have mercy on me, O Lord!

The Judge: I will be gracious to whom I will be gracious, and will show mercy on whom I will show mercy. Angels, lead away this soul to the furnace of purgation, that he may be cleansed of his vices.

SCENARIO #2 TAKES PLACE IN THE YEAR 638.

The Judge: Why, friend, did you hold and promote the wicked error that I have only one will, a divine, while having two natures, a divine and a human? Did you not see that this error is an insult to the truth of My humanity and of My mission to assume, heal, and elevate all that is in man?

Soul: But Lord, Lord, I was merely following what Pope Honorius wrote in his letter to Patriarch Sergius, where he disowned writers who spoke of "two wills." As you know, many are following this letter.

The Judge: The Church had already taught the truth about Me. The faithful knew it. Pope Honorius was derelict in his duty. His word is nothing if it contradicts the traditional teaching of the Church. Those who follow him in this matter, so far from being excused, are partakers in his unfaithfulness.

Soul: But wasn't it his fault for misleading me?

The Judge: You could and should have known better. Did you consider yourself an educated Catholic?

Soul: Well, yes, I suppose.

The Judge: You were literate at a time when few others were. You had the ability to study, and you *did* study. You knew—or could easily have known—the traditional faith of the Church.

Soul (blushing): Yes, Lord, all that you say is true.

The Judge: A successor of Pope Honorius, Pope Martin I, will show forth to all the world the unwavering faithfulness I expect of My shepherds. Martin will summon a synod to condemn Monothelitism, bravely opposing the Emperor. He will be seized, imprisoned, and exiled unto his death, and afterwards venerated as a martyr. The Third Ecumenical Council of Constantinople will ultimately discard the last vestiges of this error and condemn Honorius with words that I shall inspire on their lips: "We define that there shall be expelled from the holy Church of God and anathematized Honorius who was at one time Pope of Old Rome, because of what we found written by him to Sergius, where he in all respects followed the latter's view and confirmed his impious doctrines." Pope Leo II, endorsing the anathema, will write: "Honorius ... consented to the pollution of the unpolluted rule of the apostolic tradition, which he received from his predecessors." He will condemn him as one "who did not, as became the apostolic authority, quench the flame of heretical doctrine as it sprang up, but quickened it by his negligence." Why is it that Martin I, Leo II, and countless other popes will know and teach the truth of the Faith, when Honorius himself did not?

Soul: I cannot say, Master.

The Judge: It is because, as a matter of principle, they reject every profane novelty and "contend earnestly for the faith once delivered to the saints," as My servant Jude said. I have placed it within reach of every diligent shepherd of the flock to know and to hand on the true Faith, just as I have placed it within reach of every earnest Christian soul to receive and to embrace the same Faith unto salvation.

Soul: I see now how negligent I have been!

The Judge: Did I not condemn false prophets and false teachers in Sacred Scripture? And those who follow them?

Soul: Yes.

The Judge: Anyone who distorts the word of God as handed down in Scripture and Tradition is a false prophet. Is this not so?

Soul: Yes.

The Judge: Therefore a pope who does this is also a false prophet and teacher.

Soul: Yes, the conclusion follows.

The Judge: It is just for me to condemn you out of your own mouth. Angels, bind him hand and foot, and cast him into the outer darkness!

SCENARIO #3 TAKES PLACE IN THE YEAR 1332.

The Judge: Are you surprised to hear that countless souls of the just are already enjoying the vision of My divine glory?

Soul: I do not understand the question, Master.

The Judge: You belonged to the papal court, did you not? As a member thereof, you made a name for yourself by adopting and defending the thesis of Pope John XXII that just souls are admitted to the beatific vision only at the end of time, with the general resurrection.

Soul: Yes, I was his lawyer, and assisted him in the research that supported his position.

The Judge: His position is execrably false. The testimony of Scripture, the Fathers, the Doctors, and the constant faith of the people—all these stand in serried ranks against it. How could you have dared to aid and abet the pope in his foolish reasoning?

Soul: It seemed like a subject open to theological debate. I believe a German cardinal told me that . . .

The Judge: It is not for you to decide what is open to debate and what is not.

Soul: But what if the pope decides that something is open to debate?

The Judge: He, too, is bound by the same faith as every Christian. Indeed, he is *more* bound than all others, and must show himself stalwart in resisting every deviation, innovation, or obfuscation, be it ever so small. What may be pardoned in a lesser man may not be pardoned in the supreme shepherd.

Soul: You are saying that I should have refused to cooperate with him in this matter?

The Judge: Yes—and all the more so, the more the pope insisted on his idiosyncratic views. My loyal subjects, including the bishop Guillaume Durand, the Dominican Thomas Waleys, the Franciscan Nicholas of Lyra, Cardinal Fournier, and King Philip, valiantly resisted John's error and have suffered as a result, winning great merit for their souls. In fact, I tell you, searching the hearts of men, that before two years of time have passed upon the earth, the pope will retract his error and die repentant.

Soul: The truth is always victorious.

The Judge: It is victorious—in those who seek it and hold on to it, come what may.

Soul: What will happen after my lord dies?

The Judge: Cardinal Fournier will be elected Pope Benedict XII. Among his first acts, he will solemnly define in a papal bull the opposite of what his predecessor endeavored to teach: the souls of the just, whether immediately or after due purgation, are admitted to the beatific vision, and thereafter await the resurrection of the dead and the general judgment.

Soul: But Lord, if you had only let me live long enough to see this papal bull, I would have taken the right side!

The Judge: No, there you are wrong, My friend. Remember My parable about Dives and Lazarus? It is pertinent to your case... I know that you would have become a contumacious heretic and that your eternal punishment would have been worse. I therefore mercifully summoned you now to a lesser punishment.

Soul: I bow before your decree and accept your just sentence.

The Judge: Angels, take this lawyer and lead him to the place where he will find himself most at home—with the scribes and pharisees who changed the law of God to suit the human traditions of their cultural milieu.

These three scenarios help us to see that there are certain excuses we should never make for ourselves when it comes to adherence to Christian doctrine on faith and morals. This is *our* responsibility; we cannot abdicate it and try to put the blame on someone else.

The Catholic Church has known times of great confusion before. And although looking back we regret these periods and the wayward people who made them possible, we also gain wisdom and courage from the realization that the Church's shepherds will not always preserve the Faith intact or defend it as they should, and that the faithful have a fundamental obligation from their baptism to hold fast to the orthodox Faith, no matter what pressures are brought to bear against them.

IN ORDER TO REAP INSIGHTS TODAY FROM DIFFICULT moments in the past, we imagined three hypothetical scenarios in which souls that came to judgment in the years 366, 638, and 1332 were sentenced to punishment because of their culpable negligence in following straying shepherds. Come to think of it, the same kind of scenario just might happen today...

A soul bearing the character of the priesthood and the dignity of the episcopate is brought by angelic ministers into the presence of the King of kings and Lord of lords. A blinding splendor shines upon His countenance, light pours from the caverns of His wounds.

The Judge: Wicked servant, now stripped of your signs of ecclesiastical dignity, how dared you sow confusion and ambiguity about the crime of divorce, the fiction of "remarriage," and the sacrilege of admitting adulterers to the holy banquet of my sacrificial love?

Soul (quaking): I thought I was doing the right thing.

The Judge: Have you never read the words I spoke, reported by my trustworthy servant Matthew? "For this cause shall a man leave father and mother, and shall cleave to his wife, and they two shall be in one flesh. Therefore now they are not two, but one flesh. What therefore God hath joined together, let no man put asunder." Could I have spoken more clearly?

Soul (bolder): But sometimes those who are supposed to be one flesh separate again into two individuals, and go their separate ways. Are we not supposed to provide for their needs, too, once they are split apart?

The Judge: Christians joined in marriage cannot be split apart in My eyes. They remain one until death separates them. What I have joined together, no man has power to divide. Man fancies himself powerful because he can split the atom, and in this way he could even destroy the earth with his weapons, were I to permit him; but he cannot separate those who have been made one flesh by my will. Have not my servants John the Baptist, Thomas More, John Fisher, Blessed Peter ToRot, and many others given their lives in defense of the indissolubility of Christian marriage? Has any Doctor of My Church ever taught otherwise? Has not pope after pope upheld this truth in fidelity to My word, condemning every open or subtle deviation from it?

Soul: Truly, then, I have been deceived by those on earth who claimed to speak in your name!

The Judge: Why were you deceived? The truth is written in the Gospel—the very Gospel you were ordained to preach, in season and out of season, for the salvation of mankind. "Moses by reason of the hardness of your heart permitted you to put away your wives: but from the beginning it was not so. I say to you, that whosoever shall put away his wife, except it be for fornication, and shall marry another, committeth adultery: and he that shall marry her that is put away, committeth adultery." This I said, and this I meant. Divorce was not God's plan in the beginning. It was never God's plan. When I came among you in the flesh, I revealed that it is hardness of hearts without grace, and only this, that drives a husband to reject a wife, or a wife a husband. I suffered and died on the Cross to obtain for every human being a heart of flesh like My own: a heart able and willing to suffer and to die for one's friend, one's brother or sister, one's spouse, or parent, or child. I perpetually make this grace available to all who call upon Me. This is what you should have taught, rather than bending and twisting My words, trying to find ways to escape the severe mercy of my love, which gives all—and demands all.

Soul: Surely, Master, this teaching is too hard for men, weak as they are!

The Judge: It is too hard for men on their own. In the same Gospel, I said: "With men this is impossible, but with God all things are possible." Although I was speaking of the evangelical counsels, the same thing is true of marriage: I and I alone make it possible by My grace for spouses to love one another faithfully all their lives; I make it possible for them to welcome as many children as I am prepared to give them; I make it possible for them to bear even the worst crosses in married life—barrenness, betrayal, abuse, abandonment—for love of Me and for eternal life. The reality of this invincible grace is shown to all the world in the host of martyrs who followed my bloodstained footsteps to heavenly glory.

Soul: What about people who, in spite of their irregular situation, desperately need the help of Your sacraments?

The Judge: You are all sinners—and every one of you desperately needs the help of the sacraments if you are to overcome sin and reach My kingdom at last. But as you know from the Apostle John and from the constant teaching of My Church, there is sin that does not reject My friendship, and there is sin that does. The Church rightly calls the one venial and the other mortal. Mortal sin, unrepented and persisted in, excludes a man from My sacraments and from eternal life. A married Christian who lives sexually with another person who is not his or her original and only spouse is guilty of adultery. No true Christian has ever thought otherwise. Indeed, even the pagan Aristotle thought one could never justify adultery, or make it virtuous by changing this or that circumstance of it. He had a lot more sense than most of you on earth nowadays, which is greatly to your shame.

Soul: I am confused. Is not all this a disciplinary matter in the hands of Your Church? Was it not left up to us to determine the conditions for receiving the sacraments?

The Judge: Your confusion is as deep as the netherworld. Incidental conditions are left up to the Church: how often one may or must receive a certain sacrament, or how long one must fast before receiving it, or similar things. Essential conditions for conferring or receiving the sacraments are intrinsic to their very symbolism and reality, which come from My institution of them. You speak as if you had never studied theology!

Soul: You know where I studied, at the—

The Judge: —alas, your formation in theology was deplorably bad: superficial, incomplete, distorted by subjectivism and sentimentalism, altogether vitiated by modern prejudices. This was only partly your own fault and had much to do with the decade in which you went to school and the teachers that were visited upon you. Your pains will be duly mitigated on that account.

Soul: But Lord, Lord, is it not more merciful to let sinners have the medicine of the Eucharist?

The Judge: We come at last to the core of your reprehensible error. Do not abuse the high and sovereign name of Mercy, nor the sweet and ineffable mystery of My Body and Blood! I have mercy on the most horrible sinner if only he repents and wills to abandon his sins. I wash away his guilt with my Precious Blood and make his soul as white as wool. I hold the contrite sinner to my Heart with a love far greater than that of a mother for her newborn child, or of a husband for his beautiful bride. I nourish him with manna from heaven and water from the rock. But My mercy cannot cleanse a sinner who loves his sin. He will have the destiny he chooses for himself. If he lives in sin, sin will be his life; and if he dies in sin, sin—that is, separation from me—will be his eternity. Giving the Eucharist to such a one only heaps the burning coals of further sins upon his head.

Soul (desperate to justify itself): But we were told that it is high time for a new Church, a compassionate, caring Church that welcomes everyone.

The Judge: There is one and only one Church. I am its Head, and my Law—obedience to which is salvation—never changes. All are welcome who wish to be subject to this Law. You, on the contrary, have made a mockery of My holy religion by lulling sinners to sleep, salving their consciences, when they needed rather to be awakened to their true condition and brought to repentance. Only those who acknowledge their mortal sickness will seek healing from the divine Physician. Otherwise, they will die in their sins.

Soul: We were told to show mercy to everyone!

The Judge: Many do not know what mercy actually means. There is only one true mercy: the severe mercy of My truth, which wounds and heals in love. The scars of My wounds, which I suffered for bearing witness to the truth and for love of sinners, remain with Me forever in glory. They are proof that there is no glory without truth, no happiness without suffering, no love of neighbor without the love of God above all and before all else. Without this radical commitment to Me, "love" is only a four-letter word for selfishness.

Soul (increasingly agitated): Why—from whom—how was I to know?

The Judge: In my patience and love for mankind, I have provided countless witnesses to the truth—the inspired, inerrant, and infallible Scriptures, the consensus of the Fathers, the collective weight of the Doctors, the resounding unanimity of the Magisterium across the centuries, and, in your own lifetime, cardinals, bishops, priests, and laymen who tirelessly proclaimed the truth about marriage and the family. You have no excuse, not even the shadow of an excuse.

Soul (exhausted): Thou art just, O Lord, and Thy judgment is right.

The Judge: Archangels, lead this prince off to the place that befits him.

13

Are the "Inopportuniﬆs" of the First Vatican Council Being Vindicated?

T HE 150TH ANNIVERSARY OF THE OPENING of Vatican I on December 8, 1869, which came and went even more quietly than did the fiftieth anniversary of the going-into-effect of the *Novus Ordo Missae* on November 30, 1969,[1] prompts us to seek answers to the increasingly urgent question: Can we find a healthy way to think about the pope and the papacy, considering how much damage a certain "papolatry" has caused to the life of the Church in recent times?

It is more than a little intriguing to think about the fact that at Vatican I there was a sizable minority of bishops, with many sympathetic theologians behind them, who considered the definition of papal infallibility "inopportune" (hence their name: "inopportunists"). They did not necessarily dispute the dogmatic content; they disputed the timing of it as well as the manner in which it would be likely to be (mis)understood and (mis)applied. Indeed, this is the sole grounds on which anyone could reasonably oppose a definition of something already known to be true. For example, we know that Our Lady is the Mediatrix of All Grace and the Co-Redemptrix, that is, the one who perfectly participates in the redemption won by her Son on the Cross—*sub et cum Christo*, with and beneath Christ. It is therefore a blasphemy to dispute that these titles belong to Our Lady. But people may legitimately disagree about when and how, and even if, they ought to be officially declared by the Church.

Let us look for a moment at the benefits and liabilities of Vatican I's teaching on papal prerogatives (obviously a huge subject, but here we are concerned with larger patterns discernible over the past 150 years).

---

1 See "Why Is the Liturgical Establishment Not Celebrating the 50th Anniversary of the *Novus Ordo*?," *New Liturgical Movement*, October 28, 2019.

As regards what we might call "one-off events," the only teachings of the pope the Holy Spirit will absolutely protect are, of course, the infallible ones. As Vatican I defines, the pope enjoys the infallibility with which Christ willed to endow His Church when he is declaring a doctrine of faith or morals in the exercise of his role as supreme shepherd of the universal Church, and makes it clear that he is doing so. This is an act of the *extraordinary* Magisterium, and, as such, not likely to be easily missed when it happens—which is not very frequently. The obvious examples are the dogmatic definition of the Immaculate Conception in 1854 and of the Assumption in 1950.

But we should keep in mind that the Holy Spirit will protect the Church's *ordinary* Magisterium, and so, the general "drift" of *non*-infallible teachings over the centuries—potentially leading to a cumulatively infallible teaching, that is, something that is seen as universally taught in such a way that it cannot be mistaken—is *also* protected. Examples would include the restriction of holy orders to men and the prohibition on contraception. In fact, when Our Lord says "the gates of hell will not prevail" against the Church, He has the ordinary Magisterium more in view than the extraordinary one, since it is far more common a guide to Christian faith and life. An encyclical like *Humanae Vitae* or an apostolic letter like *Ordinatio Sacerdotalis* has a much greater immediate impact than the Marian dogmas, as sublime and central as they are.

The bishops at Vatican I thought they were erecting an effective bulwark against modernity when they defined papal infallibility, but, in point of fact, the *defining* of papal infallibility has brought about a detrimental result: the general devaluing of the Church's day-to-day teachings, since they do not rise up to the lofty level of an extraordinary act. Hence the phenomenon of liberal dissenters who say: "Apart from the two Marian dogmas, nothing popes have taught is binding on us." (It is no less true that a pope's teaching must be consistent with that of his predecessors, or else it loses its status.) I will not be so bold as to say that Vatican I should not have defined this papal prerogative, yet it does tend to distract people as they think about the meaning of Our Lord's promise to Peter.

Vatican I also declared that, in matters of governance, the pope has universal jurisdiction—something that was seen in a piecemeal way throughout Church history from early on. Yet now that the fact has been *defined*, the pope over the past 150 years has come to exercise his universal jurisdiction more extensively than is needful or helpful, pressing even beyond his real jurisdiction to being every nation's primate and every Catholic's personal spiritual director via daily meditations and tweeted messages. This is not the kind of "immediate jurisdiction" Vatican I had in mind. To be fair, they could never have imagined the reach and impact of modern media.

In regard to both teaching and governance, the reality is that the pope carries in himself the Church's ability to teach and to govern—abilities that cannot be exercised in a state of separation from the pope. Our Lord's promise was that the Church would not fail in its teaching and governance in union with Peter the foundation, which only obliquely addresses the fact that Peter will not fail when acting solo.

To take Peter's solo actions as the focus when pondering Our Lord's promise distorts the nature of the promise and the role of the papacy. We end up simultaneously underestimating Peter's teaching role (by limiting it to infallible statements) and overestimating his governance (by pushing it to the details of life in every parish).

Vatican I, in a way, seems to have led to a doubly ironic result: on the one hand, the pope is frequently exalted above the very Church that makes him what he is, considers himself free to depart from the teaching and holy example of his predecessors, and encroaches almost continually on the God-given office and responsibilities of his brother bishops, while on the other hand, his ability to teach on important matters of faith and morals has become diluted and inefficacious owing to a flood of excessive and often trivial verbiage, broadcast 24/7 around the globe, because commenting on everything is somehow seen as "expected" of him. The pope is, at once, far greater than ever, and far more negligible.

What is necessary, above all, is to recover the properly ecclesial and episcopal context of the papacy, so that we see the pope as an officer of the Church, under the same twin measure of orthodoxy— that is, right teaching and right worship—as every other Catholic, and not as the Church's lord and master.

Since Vatican I defines the pope to have "that infallibility which the divine Redeemer willed his Church to enjoy in defining doctrine concerning faith or morals," it follows that the authority of popes and the authority of ecumenical councils—or of bishops taken all together as witnesses to the Faith and teachers of their flocks—is essentially identical.

Note that infallibility is a negative guarantee: it means freedom from error when defining matters of faith and morals. Therefore, a pope who teaches *ex cathedra* and a council that makes *de fide* declarations and anathematizes their contrary errors are alike teaching infallibly—that is, without possibility of error, although neither is guaranteed to have given the best or most complete formulation that could admit of no possible improvement or augmentation. It follows, moreover, that a pope or a council that teaches *without* signifying such an intention to declare and bind all Christians is teaching with magisterial authority, but without such a guarantee of infallibility. In other words, a pope or council may be in error when not teaching infallibly (this is almost a tautological statement).

Beyond this negative guarantee for the papacy, the worldwide episcopacy enjoys a *positive* guarantee that the deposit of faith will never perish within it. The Oath against Modernism expresses it thus: "the charism of truth, which certainly is, was, and always will be in *the succession of the episcopacy* from the apostles." In that way, the body of bishops enjoys a positive privilege that the pope, taken in isolation, lacks.

As two scholars explained it to me in a personal communication:

> This union of the positive and negative guarantees, absent in merely papal teaching, is why Bishop Vincent Gasser said in his *Relatio* at Vatican I that "the most solemn judgment of the Church in matters of faith and morals is and always will be the judgment of an ecumenical council, in which the Pope passes judgment together with the bishops of the Catholic world who meet and judge together with him." Conversely, this is why the Council of Florence felt the need to justify the Holy See's unilateral adoption of the *Filioque* as arising "from imminent need." The implication is that the Holy See should *not* define unilaterally except from imminent need.

To repeat: both papal and conciliar teaching can be in error (that is, are fallible) precisely when they do not officially and expressly engage the highest level of authority that pertains to them, viz., establishing doctrine in a definitive manner, which will be signified by language indicating that it is being taught as pertaining to the Catholic faith and must be held by all under pain of exclusion from the body of Christ.

The papal encyclical as a genre was invented by Benedict XIV in the eighteenth century, but the first time a pope addressed the universal church without exercising infallibility (as understood by theologians until that time) was when Gregory XVI condemned Lamennais in 1832 while choosing not to issue censures. If this is correct, it could be argued that the *routine* issuing of fallible teaching to the universal Church is an inappropriate use of the papal office, which eclipses the functions of the diocesan bishop.[2]

The hypertrophism of papal authority in the past 150 years has had the unintended side-effect of greatly diminishing the stature of bishops, to the point where they seem incapable of proclaiming the orthodox faith or taking on heretics without the pope leading the way or even providing the script. The ultimate *reductio ad absurdum* is the striking spectacle of today: some 5,100 Catholic bishops, the vast majority of whom appear to be incapable of breathing a word against a notorious manufacturer of scandals and a multipronged heretic.

Let's contrast the situation with the ringing statements of the Lateran Synod of A. D. 649, still in the heroic age of the Church Fathers:

> If anyone . . . does not reject and anathematize in his soul
> and with his lips *all those* whom the holy, catholic and

---

2   John Lamont notes: "Papal teaching authority was exercised from the Middle Ages onwards largely by issuing theological censures. Not all these censures were the censure of heresy, so not every such censure was a defining of doctrine, but the issuing of a censure was understood to be an infallible teaching act. That is why theologians until the nineteenth century assumed that the pope either taught infallibly or made a statement as a private doctor. The book on this is Bruno Neveu's outstanding *L'erreur et son juge: Remarques sur les censures doctrinales à l'époque moderne*. When it came to condemning Lamennais censures were not issued; see the brothers Le Guillou's excellent book *La condamnation de Lamennais*. After this, theological censure ceased to be used by popes. They either wrote encyclicals or on a couple of occasions made infallible definitions in apostolic constitutions. I asked Abbé Claude Barthe about why this was and he said he did not know. It was a major change for the worse that has not been explained or really investigated" (private correspondence).

apostolic Church of God . . . rejects and anathematizes as
most abominable heretics, together with all their impious writings down to the last detail—that is, Sabellius,
Arius . . . and in brief, all the remaining heretics . . . [i]f
anyone therefore . . . does not reject and anathematize all
those most impious doctrines of their heresy, and those
matters that have been impiously written by anyone in
their favor or in explanation of them . . . *let such a person
be condemned.*[3]

Could this passage be written off, Protestant-style, as one more
example of how uppity and intolerant the Catholic Church had
become after several centuries of public prominence and pastoral
pretensions? No, that trick won't work. It was St. Paul and St.
John, whose apostolic credentials no sane Christian calls into
question, who first gave us the model of condemning heretics *by
name* and *in no uncertain terms.* In 2 Timothy and 3 John, we find
the following seven names spelled out: Phygelus, Hermogenes,
Hymenaeus, Philetus, Demas, Alexander, and Diotrophes. Their
names stand in Scripture for no other reason than to provide a
model of how such people should be dealt with.

According to the entire history and practice of the Faith, one
must confront the *man* who is a heretic and condemn that man's
doctrines and the man *alike.* It is not enough to condemn errors
without singling out those who originate or promote or defend
them. That is the great weakness of all those who will not *name*
Pope Francis as a source of evils, but are content to gesture toward
"problems," "errors," "confusions," and "mistakes." It is not only not
uncharitable to name names; it is uncharitable not to name names.

Instead, the Church in our times fosters a culture in which
each individual may assert whatever doctrine he supposes sounds
good to him, trading his idea with that of someone with whom he
disagrees, in an everlasting dialectic until kingdom come. Such a
culture is reminiscent of the position of Protestants, who, having
only the private authority of their personal interpretations of
Scripture, lack a body of teaching based on the Deposit of Faith
and an ecclesial hierarchy to which appeal can be made and from
which answers can be handed down. Trading doctrines like this,

---

3   Canon 18; Denzinger-Hünermann 518–522.

in a great give-and-take of chummy tolerance, *is not and never has been Catholic.* It might best be termed "Anglican."

The Catholic way—authoritative proclamation and clear condemnation—is the way of Christ, the apostles, and the Fathers. It was the way of the Church until Vatican II, when John XXIII signified a rupture with past practice in *Gaudet Mater Ecclesia*: now the medicine of an optimistic mercy would be delivered to men of Pelagian good will. This new method, heavy on sentiment and light on truth, combined with unchecked hyperpapalism and episcopal diminution, results in a dysfunctional ecclesiastical body.

14

Could a Heretical Pope Remain in Office?

C AN A POPE BE A FORMAL HERETIC BUT still somehow continue in his office (although he will be prevented from declaring heresy *ex cathedra*)? In an article at *OnePeterFive*, Eric Sammons makes a compelling case that the answer is "yes."[1]

St. Robert Bellarmine laid out the various possible scenarios well, but there are two objections to the way he reasoned about them. On the one hand, his argument against the possibility that "the pope could be a heretic" is not tight: it would be a terrible trial, he says. But God's providence could allow even a terrible trial for a time, so long as it did not damage the Church beyond recovery. On the other hand, his argument for the possibility that "the Church could simply recognize the fact of the pope's abdication" on account of heresy encounters insurmountable practical difficulties: by the time the Church has a formal heretic as a pope, she most likely also lacks the highly virtuous churchmen necessary to carry out such a maneuver. So it seems more reasonable to conclude that the pope could be even a formal heretic.

An obvious objection is that the Church has said no formal heretic can occupy an ecclesiastical office, as found in the 1917 Code of Canon Law: "Any office becomes vacant upon the fact and without any declaration by tacit resignation recognized by the law itself if a cleric: . . . 4. Publicly defects from the Catholic faith." But this is a principle of law, not a principle inherent in the natures of things. The commentators say it is "incongruous" that a heretic should occupy such an office, not that it is impossible in itself.

The reason it is not impossible for a heretic to occupy an ecclesial office is that the Church is defined not only by belief and loyalty, but also by place and time. Someone who has defected from the Church's belief and therefore ceased to be Catholic in the most important sense can still, in the stupidly physical sense

---

1   See "Is Francis the Pope?," *OnePeterFive*, October 29, 2019.

of the word, occupy an ecclesiastical office: he can sit in a room in the Vatican or in a bishop's estate, and he can write on official letterhead, and so on. One could approach him and say, "Excuse me, but since you are no longer a Catholic, you should leave the room." But he will say, "How dare you say I am no longer a Catholic?"

Formal heretics, despite their formal heresy, have rarely admitted to being no longer in the fold. And as long as no one else can occupy the office, and the people subject to that office have no power to act, this squatter in the office wields a *de facto* authority. It is incongruous that someone outside the Catholic faith continues to tell people what to do in the Church—it is, in fact, rather like someone who does not belong to a family having absolute power over the family. But it is not impossible.

In actual practice, therefore, formal heretics *have* occupied ecclesiastical offices, until someone with authority to do so (and, often enough, with thugs to back him up) insists that they leave. So the current Code of Canon Law repeats the old canon: "The following are removed from ecclesiastical office by virtue of the law itself: . . . 2. One who has publicly defected from the Catholic faith." But it merely acknowledges the reality of the situation when it adds: "The removal mentioned in nn. 2 and 3 can be insisted upon only if it is established by a declaration of the competent authority." True, this declaration is a mere recognition of *fact*, but for the automatic removal from office to have *juridical* effect, the recognition must come from a competent authority.

Therein lies the difficulty when it comes to the Petrine office. This principle stated by Canon Law can have its effect only if we can find someone authorized to say, in an official way, that the pope is a formal heretic. In any case, it is tricky to get a canon law case up against the man who has absolute power over canon law.

This leaves us with the practical difficulty of getting together a contingent of men somehow either authorized or competent and virtuous enough to "merely recognize" the pope's *de facto* abdication. Pending that, no one else can occupy the office, and everyone under him continues under an obligation of obeying (according to a correct notion of obedience: one obeys unless commanded to act against the known truth held with a good conscience). This is to say that, in some real yet irritating sense, he still occupies the office despite having rejected it in some important way.

Most authors say that a notorious and formal heretic can hold ecclesiastical office despite the fact that heresy separates one from the Church; but they will add that the occupancy of such office is made possible by extraordinary jurisdiction supplied by the Church—which some interpret to mean "supplied by the pope." If this were true, then a manifestly and notoriously heretical pope could not supply his own jurisdiction, so the usual basis for saying that a heretical cleric can retain office would not apply in the case of such a pope. In other words, he would be *worse off* than all other bishops. This seems counterintuitive at first but would make sense from the vantage of his office being the first and most important and therefore not capable of retaining someone who ought to believe and act as the visible head of the Church on Earth.

However, this claim about supplied jurisdiction masks a secret papolatry. Since it is the very nature of the Church that demands the existence of the papal office—in other words, since *the pope is not first, simply speaking*, but, as a member of the Church, exercises an office *of* the Church and *for* the Church—the pope gets his jurisdiction *from* the Church. The Church is the first and abiding reality with and under Christ, and the pope is consequent to that reality. There are other offices within the Church that are consequent to the Church *simultaneously with the pope's office*—that is, there are other offices consequent to the Church that are not consequent to the pope. Hence, it is truer to say a heretical cleric can retain office because of jurisdiction supplied by the nature of the Church.

The Lord does not allow any evil except for the sake of some good, and in the case of the just whom the Lord loves, that good will be growth in virtue, achievement of sanctity, and everlasting glory, together with the conversion or punishment of their persecutors. I hope and believe, as part of my basic act of faith in God, that every evil the Church suffers will somehow advance her well-being in the end. That such may be the case in our present mighty trial, I daily beg of the crucified yet risen Lord, adding my prayers to the incense of those martyrs recounted in Revelation 6, and adding my cry to theirs: "How long?"

MANY THINK THAT THE IDEA OF A POPE BEING overturned for heresy is utterly unthinkable. Yet it is the sort of scenario that was patiently and thoroughly discussed by many great Catholic theologians, especially during and after the Great Western Schism, and even more during the Reformation period. The possibility of a heretical pope and the right way to resist him were never "forbidden topics" in former centuries.

Case study: the Portuguese Jesuit Francisco Leytam (1631–1716) dedicated to Cosimo III de Medici an enormous tome entitled *The Impenetrable Shield of the Dignity of the Papacy* (in the original: *Impenetrabilis Pontificiae Dignitatis Clypeus*). It had all the usual recognitions and permissions for publication.[2] This treatise dedicates a considerable section to how a heretical pope is deposed. In Section IX, Leytam considers the case in which the elected pope "does not respect the Sacraments or does other things contrary to the definitions of faith made either by Councils or by other popes preceding him."[3] Leytam argues, citing authorities, that in this case "he may be deposed by the Church" [*potest deponi ab Ecclesia*]. The reason he furnishes is worth careful attention:

> because those sinful precepts against that which is defined by faith in the Church are external signs which signify the internal disposition of a heretic: for heresy is not only signified in words but also in actions: whence if the pope does not wish to amend, he may be declared to be a heretic, in which case he will be censured immediately by Christ and deposed by Him: and then he would not be pope but a private person able to be punished by the Church.[4]

One wishes to shake today's hyperpapalists awake with the caffeinated message that Catholic theology is a lot bolder and goes a lot deeper than the tidy syllogisms of Jesuit neoscholastic manuals or the well-intentioned musings, more sentimental than coherent, of Protestant converts from the twentieth century.

---

2   A digitized copy is available on Google Books.

3   §77: "ne observarentur Sacramenta, & ut aliquid fieret contra definitiones de fide tam in Conciliis, quam extra, ab aliis Pontificibus antecessoribus factas."

4   §78: "quia ille praeceptiones iniquae contra id, quod de fide est in Ecclesia definitum, sunt signa externa significativa interni affectus haeretici: haeresis enim non solum significatur verbis sed factis: undè si Papa ab his non vult emendari, potest declarari, ut haereticus, & censebitur immediatè à Christo deponi: & tunc jam ut non Papa, sed ut persona privata potest ab Ecclesia puniri, ut suo loco dictum est."

When the Open Letter of April 2019 accusing Pope Francis of heresy was first published,[5] I recall that one reader objected that the seven heretical propositions identified by the Letter were "all about sex and Islam." Leaving aside Islam, which is poised to overrun Christianity in its historical regions, we could respond: So what if the propositions are primarily about sexual morality? That is the main arena in which the devil has seduced the modern world and the modern Church. Yes, there are worse errors, but nothing is more like quicksand or tarpits than sins against the sixth and ninth commandments. The Open Letter focused on statements that are obviously heretical (which they are), repeatedly said in important contexts, and backed up with actions. Many of Francis's other doctrinal errors have been uttered in homilies or interviews, which carry just about zero magisterial weight (recall that it was a medieval pope, John XXII, who used the vehicle of papal homilies to articulate his errors about the afterlife).[6] "Denzinger-Bergoglio" already exists online for documenting hundreds of such deviations; the authors of the Open Letter confined themselves to the "smoking guns."

If Christians in earlier centuries (especially the first five centuries) were perhaps too quick to label "heresy" any opinion they couldn't immediately recognize as familiar and to brand as a "heretic" anyone with whom they disagreed, today we are vastly too elaborate and slow in pegging as heresy an opinion at variance with Scripture or Tradition, or identifying as a heretic someone who manifestly is one. Take Pierre Teilhard de Chardin, S. J.: how many people would wince to hear him called a heretic? And yet he manifestly was, a thousand times over.[7] We can become victims of our partialities, crippled by our caution, stifled by our pseudo-scholasticism.

The words of Venerable Bartholomew Holzhauser (1613-1658) predicted a future of logic-choppers, of Scholars of the Law, who would fashion sophistries to avoid adhering to Catholic tradition and replace it with their novelties:

> They will ridicule Christian simplicity; they will call it folly and nonsense, but they will have the highest regard for advanced knowledge, and for the skill by which the axioms

---

5   See Lamont and Pierantoni, *Defending the Faith*, 129–55.

6   See de Mattei, *Love for the Papacy*, 40–44.

7   See "Teilhard de Chardin: Model of Ambiguity for a Future Pope," *OnePeterFive*, January 16, 2019.

of the law, the precepts of morality, the Holy Canons and religious dogmas are clouded by senseless questions and elaborate arguments. As a result, no principle at all, however holy, authentic, ancient, and certain it may be, will remain free of censure, criticism, false interpretation, modification, and delimitation by man.[8]

Holzhauser's words describe what has transpired under Pope Francis: the Christian simplicity that holds fast to the truth and identifies error, deviation, and corruption is attacked by the self-appointed knights of the papacy who care nothing for holy, authentic, ancient, and certain principles. We must let them go, for we probably cannot persuade them to think or act otherwise, and make sure that we ourselves maintain and proclaim the truth of Christ and His Church, which no one—not even an angel from God, *a fortiori* not a pope of Rome—can alter.

---

8   See "Ven. Bartholomew Holzhauser on the Here and Now," *Creative Minority Report*, September 11, 2015.

15

Why Sedevacantism
Is No Solution

THERE HAVE ALWAYS BEEN A SMALL NUM-
ber of Catholics since the Second Vatican Council who,
looking at the apostasy, heresy, impiety, and desolation
widespread in the Church, have reached the conclusion that
there is not a legitimate pope seated on the throne of Peter.
Such Catholics are called "sedevacantists," from the Latin for
"empty seat."

Sedevacantists come in many varieties, but generally they hold
that there has been no valid pope since the death of Pope Pius XII
in October 1958. "Sedeprivationists," on the other hand, maintain
that all the popes of the past sixty-four years have been popes
"materially" but not "formally": they have been appointed by God
to serve as popes, but they have refused to accept the duties of
their office and have thus paralyzed their functionality. This view
is held by a minority even within the minority.

One can sympathize with the lamentations and dismay of
Catholics who are appalled by the infidelities of churchmen after
the Council, but the position they advocate is untenable.

The real root of sedevacantism is ultramontanism—the very
problem under which we have been suffering since the *First* Vatican
Council. Because none of the popes after Pius XII has lived up
to the heights of doctrinal perfection and personal sanctity that
ultramontanists unreasonably expect in the Vicar of Christ, they
are therefore tempted to conclude that these popes must not
really be popes. But what is needed, instead, is a gritty realism
that recognizes how seriously popes can mess up.

Just *how* seriously is something that cannot be spelled out in
advance of history showing it to us. I'm sure prior to Honorius
there would have been people saying "A pope can never endorse
heresy." Well, along comes Honorius and upsets *that* apple-cart. (He's
not the only one to upset it, either.) Sure, all kinds of elaborate
defenses and distinctions can be made to show that Honorius or

the other doctrinally dubious popes did not attempt to enforce heresy on the faithful by an *ex cathedra* pronouncement (etc.), but this does not modify the fact that a successor of Peter and a Vicar of Christ can, in fact, think erroneously about matters of faith and morals, and utter those erroneous opinions in a non-binding manner. Knowing that this is indeed possible is enormously helpful when confronted with a pope like Francis, who is swimming in the deep end of error on all manner of things.

Maybe another person in Church history might have said: "Christ would only choose for his Vicar a man *worthy* of the office." Well, along comes the Dark Ages and we have simoniacs, nepotists, murderers, fornicators, and warlords occupying the throne of Peter. Just as infallibility doesn't attach to most papal utterances, neither does impeccability attach to papal incumbents.

Needless to say, Pope Francis is now pushing the bounds of papal deviancy far beyond anything we have ever seen before—and instead of denying this crisis, theologians need to accept it as an invitation to re-think, from the very foundations, the specious ultramontanist narrative that has been operative for the past 150 years or more. It invites all Catholics to recommit themselves to the Faith of our Fathers.

The basic problem with sedevacantism is that it is a "tidy" explanation that does not actually admit the depth of the problem—and also has no solution for it. What I mean by the first part of this claim is that it is easier for a sedevacantist to dismiss sixty years of "bad popes" measured against a Platonic standard than to face up to the horrifying reality of a true pope who is nevertheless a heretic or a bad man. What I mean by the second part is this: If there haven't been popes for decades, how are we ever supposed to get a new pope? Will he drop from the sky? None of the cardinals would be legitimate cardinal-electors; indeed, the entire hierarchy of the Church would be fatally compromised.

No, the truth is that we have a pope and will always have a pope. The Church will never fail to have a visible head, so that the visible Church may reflect the full stature of Christ, who is made up of head and members. Obviously, there are periods in between pontificates (usually quite short) as a decision is reached about who will succeed the deceased pope, but for Our Lord's promises to Peter to hold good, such a popeless period must be limited, temporary, and easily brought to an end. The longest conclave in history was the one that elected Clement IV, which met from November 1268 to September 1271. Three years, although frightfully long, is still rather short compared to the sixty years demanded by the sedevacantist position.

I shall be blunt about this: If the Catholic Church has not had a pope for over sixty years, then the promises of Christ have failed, and this Church is not the true Church. Moreover, if the Catholic Church is not the true Church, there *is* no true Church, since no other institution has nearly as good a claim on this title (and I include in this assessment the Eastern Orthodox). Since we know, as a matter of divine and Catholic faith, that the Church cannot be merely invisible and cannot be lacking an earthly head who is the image of the heavenly head and the successor of Peter in the college of the Apostles, we should have no difficulty as baptized members of Christ confessing that we have a pope and will always have a pope—namely, the one who is recognized and acknowledged as such by the worldwide episcopate and the body of the faithful *in genere*.

Yes: *habemus papam*. He just happens to be a very bad one, by every standard ever applied to assess papacies in the past 2,000 years.

Here is a letter I received from a lifelong Catholic in "anguish" over the state of the Church. The letter is followed by my response. I sense that many people find themselves in the same situation, feeling the same confusion and betrayal. The pain and the shock Catholics are experiencing today is understandable. What is most important, however, is that we not lose heart.

DEAR SIR:

We don't know each other, but I have read your work in *Latin Mass* magazine, and see that you are an intelligent and faithful traditional Catholic. That is why I feel moved to write to you.

I can't begin to put into this message the anguish I feel over the state of the Church, but I am hoping and praying you might have some insight for me. I am 62 years old, a lifelong Catholic who discovered the traditional Latin Mass about 5 years ago. This began a journey that led to the realization that for 50+ years, under the reign of the "spirit of Vatican II," I have been lied to or at least misled about the authentic teachings of the Church.

I am trying to make sense of this crisis, and in particular, trying to find out "who," so to speak, I should align myself with: a good local Novus Ordo priest who also offers the Latin Mass? The FSSP? The SSPX? Sedevacantists? The list goes on and on.

What frustrates me even more is that I beg God for clarity. "Lord, who should I align myself with? Who speaks your truth? Please, I am your son begging you for help. Please." But I don't seem to receive any answer to my prayer. How can He allow this to happen to His Church? Is this really the worst crisis ever in the history of the Church? (That's a real question I would like an answer to.) Why do I have to live during this time?

The greatest lie of the last 50 years, in my opinion—that God is all merciful, while nothing is said about His right to our faith and adoration, and the demands of His justice; every funeral is a canonization; there are no consequences to sin—has negatively affected my own life, as I strayed this way and that, due to lack of instruction and guidance.

Can you offer me any direction? Thank you so much.

Sincerely yours,
A Demoralized Catholic

DEAR BROTHER IN CHRIST:

I understand the pain and the shock of these realizations. Although I am younger, I too grew up with the fashionable postconciliar "Catholicism" and had to find my way out of it, by dint of study, experience, and miraculous good luck—or what looked like good luck, since it was really the providence of a merciful God. The Lord has been gracious to me, and to you, by showing us the beauty and depth of Catholic tradition. Whether this discovery comes early in our lives, or much later, or even at the very end, we should bless the Lord for rescuing us from sin, error, ignorance, mediocrity, and sloth. Remember the parable about the servants who are hired every hour throughout the day, and all receive the same reward for their labor.

Many others are also going through what you are going through. Thanks be to God an ever-growing number of our fellow Catholics are coming around to seeing things in the Church as they really are. There is both sobriety and hope in that knowledge. When we ask "Why has all this happened?," we receive from Scripture the one answer that is always true of every age: the Lord permits false prophets in order to test the love of His own (cf. Deut. 13:1–3). Those whom He loves, He chastens (cf. Heb. 12:6). He purifies us as gold in the furnace (Prov. 17:3). "I will turn My hand against you; I will thoroughly purge your dross; I will remove all your impurities" (Is. 1:25). Without some kind of systematic purification, whether here or hereafter, we would not be prepared for eternal life. The Lord therefore uses even our sins, when we repent of them, to bring about this purgation of self-love and disordered attachments.

You mention the abuse of the fair name of God's mercy. Sadly, this is true. What many fail to see is that it is inherent in God's mercy to *call us to conversion,* daily repentance, taking up our cross and following in His footsteps.

Sometimes our particular prayers are not answered in the way we are hoping or expecting, because we do not get a "customized" response, so to speak; it seems God is ignoring us or remaining sealed up in His distant silence. But this is not true. The first and most important belief of Christians—I would go so far as to say it is the belief that *makes* us Christians—is expressed incomparably well by St. John of the Cross: "In giving us His Son, His only Word (for He possesses no other), the Father spoke everything to us at once in this sole Word—and He has no more to say...because what He spoke before to the prophets in parts, He has now spoken all at once by giving us *the All* Who is His Son." Every prayer we make receives its definitive answer in Jesus Christ Himself. *He* is God's *yes* to us (2 Cor. 1:20).

This is why we put the crucifix everywhere: "The life I now live in the flesh I live by faith in the Son of God, who loved me and gave himself for me" (Gal. 2:20). The traditional liturgy brings forcefully to the eyes of our heart this "faith in the Son of God," and His sacrifice *for me.*

Christ is the crucified and glorified Savior, and His Church, being His bride who shares intimately in His life, will also have both a crucified and a glorified appearance during her history. Sometimes she is asked to go through deep suffering, as in the age of martyrs in ancient Roman times, or the age of unbelief today; sometimes she is permitted to radiate with glory as the transfigured Christ upon Mount Tabor, as in the Middle Ages, or, on a much smaller scale, in faithful monasteries and convents where the holiness of Christ is reproduced in earnest.

As a philosopher, I am professionally inclined to skepticism towards extreme statements or positions, and I am always looking for *strong* arguments. This is why sedevacantism is a non-starter for me. Moreover, I admire much about Archbishop Lefebvre, do not consider the Society of St. Pius X to be in formal schism, and applaud the good works they are doing (for example, how many dioceses are building thoroughly Catholic retirement communities and nursing homes, as the SSPX are doing?); but I remain concerned about some of the theological writing I have read from their authors, and fear that some of them have a mentality that is *materially* schismatic. In short, their situation is irregular.[1] We should always be grateful that the ancient tradition is thriving in communities like the Priestly Fraternity of St. Peter and the Institute of Christ the King Sovereign Priest.

I *do* believe we are in the worst crisis in Church history, but it is not the first time that all looked bleak. Reading the *Roman Martyrology,* or John Henry Newman on the Arian crisis of the fourth century, is enough to make one's hair stand on end. The Lord has always delivered His Church from her external *and* internal persecutors. I have no reason whatsoever to doubt Our Lord's words that He is with us always, even to the end of time, and that the Church He founded will not be overcome by the gates of hell (cf. Mt. 28:20; Mt. 16:18), nor St. John's testimony that the faithful are anointed with the knowledge of the truth (1 Jn. 2:20). I do not doubt for a moment that the Faith as taught in all the traditional catechisms, and above all at the Council of Trent, is the true Faith, and that no one, not even Pope Francis, can alter this adamantine fact. For that reason, I am at peace remaining in the Catholic Church, worshiping with her traditional rites, adhering to her time-honored doctrine, working out my salvation in fear and trembling (cf. Phil. 2:12), and praying for the conversion of her hierarchy—or for their replacement with better shepherds, as the Lord may will it.

---

1   This does not, of course, mean that Catholics may not attend their chapels: see "Is It Ever Okay to Take Shelter in an SSPX Mass?," *OnePeter-Five,* April 3, 2019.

We do not choose when we enter this world, nor are we authorized to choose when we shall leave it; the Lord alone is the ruler of life and death. Knowing all things to the last detail, He willed that we should live at just this time. He has done us the honor, one might say, of summoning us into His service at a critical moment in the fortunes of His kingdom on earth, and He will equip us with every grace we need to serve Him faithfully in our station, however humble and insignificant it may seem. "He hath put down the mighty from their seat, and hath exalted the humble" (Lk. 1:52).

Do not lose heart. Christ has overcome the world (cf. Jn. 16:33), and His grace is still available to us in the Church for our salvation, and always will be.

Yours in Christ,
Dr. Kwasniewski

16

The Shepherds We Have and the Shepherds We Need

"WAIL, YE SHEPHERDS, AND CRY; AND wallow yourselves in the dust, ye leaders of the flock: for the days of your slaughter are fully come. And I will break you in pieces, and ye shall fall like a precious vessel" (Jer. 25:34-35).

Although he lived over 2,500 years ago, the prophet Jeremiah speaks powerfully to our situation, as pointedly as if he were alive and writing at this moment. The book of his life and sayings exemplifies how "the word of God is living and effectual, and more piercing than any two-edged sword; and reaching unto the division of the soul and the spirit, of the joints also and the marrow, and is a discerner of the thoughts and intents of the heart" (Heb. 4:12). As Jeremiah himself says: "Is not my word like fire, and like a hammer that breaks the rock in pieces?" (Jer. 23:29).

Nor should we be surprised at this. The Old Testament is not just about the Israelites. Since the Church is the new Israel (cf. Gal. 6:16), the Old Testament is also about *us*, insofar as *we* are faithful or unfaithful to the new covenant made in the Blood of the Lamb, the Messiah, the Holy One of Israel, and inasmuch as *we* obey or disobey His commandments (Jn. 14:15; 1 Jn. 2:4).

So the basic pattern we see etched into almost every page of the Old Testament—fidelity to the covenant ends in God's blessing and support, infidelity in His curses and wrath—remains valid until the end of human history. In fact, is anything more obvious than that the Catholic Church today is experiencing just those curses that always accompany infidelity, abuse of trust, abuse of power, and the violence done to our theological, spiritual, cultural, and liturgical patrimony? God is faithful to His promises, and His promises include not only blessings but punishments. He *guarantees* that for sin, there will always be punishment, even as He *guarantees* with the price of the precious Blood of Jesus that there will always be salvation for those who repent of their sins.

The harsh prophecies of Jeremiah, like the consoling prophecies of Isaiah, are fulfilled again and again down through the ages in the Church founded by Christ. We in the twenty-first century happen to be living in a time in which the evil of churchmen, of the wolves in sheep's clothing, seems vastly to outweigh the good; when "the Israel of God," that is, the Church (cf. Gal. 6:16), seems hell-bent on turning its back to the Lord and the religion He has revealed; when the people have been lured into the worship of false gods and carried away captive by a pagan empire; when the once-beautiful vineyard of Catholicism has been devastated, ravaged by wild beasts, reduced to wild disarray. "Many shepherds have destroyed my vineyard, they have trodden my portion under foot, they have made my pleasant portion a desolate wilderness. They have made it a desolation; it mourneth unto me, being desolate; the whole land is made desolate" (Jer. 12:10-11).

What, according to Jeremiah, is the problem? "The shepherds are become brutish, and have not inquired of the Lord: therefore they have not prospered, and all their flocks are scattered" (Jer. 10:21). In a word, the fault is worldliness, accommodation to the mentality of the world. Hallowed ascetical practices by which Catholics sought to thwart the disordered concupiscence of the flesh—fasting, abstinence, vigils, kneeling, and other bodily penances—were chucked out the window that John XXIII innocently "opened up" at Vatican II. The result would not have been difficult to predict, for shepherd and flock alike. Instead of aspiring to heavenly goods, shepherds allowed themselves to become immersed in the things of the world and of the flesh.

Worldliness necessarily chokes off prayer, liturgy, the glorification of God, and a life of strict discipline and virtue. No spiritual prosperity can result from such infidelity; the flock are scattered into disbelief and dismay. "Woe unto the shepherds that destroy and scatter the sheep of my pasture! saith the Lord....Ye have scattered my flock, and driven them away, and have not visited them; behold, I will visit upon you the evil of your doings" (Jer. 23:1-2).

The prophet clearly indicates that this profane or mundane mentality cannot help invading the very sanctuary of the Church, as we have seen in a thousand ways. The shepherds have abused their own positions of authority, flexing muscles of power: "Their course is evil, and their might is not right; for both prophet and priest are profane; yea, in my house have I found their wickedness, saith the Lord. Wherefore their way shall be unto them as slippery places in the darkness: they shall be driven on, and fall therein; for I will bring evil upon them, even the year of their visitation" (Jer. 23:10–12). The moment of divine visitation is coming for each shepherd, one by one—whether it be initiated by civil courts or ecclesiastical courts, whether it occurs on the stage of this world or only on the day of death, before "the dread judgment seat of Christ" (in the words of the Byzantine Divine Liturgy).

As Bronwen McShea shows in her brilliant article "Bishops Unbound,"[1] the past two centuries have seen a centralization of ecclesiastical power in the hands of bishops and the pope, like nothing ever before seen in the history of the Catholic Church. Prior to this turn towards unification, concentration, and exclusivity, the Church was far more diversified in its "power base": the laity, primarily in its princes, aristocrats, and guilds, and the clergy in their cathedral chapters and associations, co-determined the manner in which the Church was governed, the policies that were implemented, the decisions that were reached. Now, we suffer under a regime in which there is no effective check on the absolute authority of the shepherds. If they are saintly, we can breathe a sigh of relief and give thanks. But if they become corrupted—and especially when the pope and the papal curia become corrupted—laity and lower clergy have no earthly recourse, no way to prevent or escape the rape and pillage.

To the extent that this is true, we know that we have recourse to God alone, and we must therefore beg Him all the more, with earnest pleas and tears, to rescue His people from abusive shepherds. He will heed our prayers, He will rescue us in due season. Once again, God speaks through Jeremiah: "I myself will fight against you," He says to His unfaithful ones, "with an outstretched hand and with a strong arm, even in anger, and in wrath, and in great indignation" (Jer. 21:5). We do not know the day or the hour, but we can be certain that He *will* fight against the shepherds who provoke Him to wrath.

Is this the only message we find in Jeremiah—one of gloom and doom, so to speak? No, not at all. For this prophet as for every prophet in Sacred Scripture, the final word is one of hope. Speaking of His own people, the Lord says: "Behold, I will bring

---

1   In the January 2019 issue of *First Things*; also available online.

it health and cure, and I will cure them; and I will reveal unto them abundance of peace and truth. And I will cause the captivity of Judah and the captivity of Israel to return, and will build them, as at the first" (Jer. 33:6–7).

The gates of hell shall never prevail, not now, nor at any time in the future—but the Word of the Lord shall prevail over a rock that has dared to set itself up in rivalry to the Rock, Jesus Christ.

"The Lord entered her and became a servant; the Word entered her, and became silent within her; thunder entered her and his voice was still; the Shepherd of all entered her; he became a Lamb in her, and came forth bleating."

Thus writes St. Ephrem the Syrian, a deacon and Doctor of the Church, in his *Hymns on the Nativity*. The Eastern Orthodox English composer John Tavener (1944–2013) set this text powerfully to music in his 1990 choral work *Thunder Entered Her*.

St. Ephrem helps himself freely to the paradoxes of the great feast of Christmas. How can a Lord be a servant? How can a Word become silent? How can the voice of thunder be still? How can a Shepherd become a lamb?

Only God can accomplish such mighty deeds, because He indeed is Lord *of all*—so great, as Pope Benedict XVI said, that He can become small without ceasing to be great.[2] The Word is so dense with meaning, so ineffable and unfathomable, that silence befits it better than a discourse, even if we can never cease proclaiming these wonderful deeds. The thunder and lightning of Sinai are the signs of the presence of the one who is Law and Love, the "still, soft voice" that speaks in man's conscience. The Shepherd of all foreknows and encloses the lambs in His arms, and has the power and the willingness to be among them as one of them: "that which He was not He took up, while that which He was He remained."

At the Mass for the Imposition of the Pallium, Conferral of the Fisherman's Ring, and Inauguration of the Pontificate on Sunday, April 24, 2005, Pope Benedict XVI preached the first of his countless memorable papal homilies that form a body of wisdom to which Catholics will be looking back for centuries,

---

2 See Homily of His Holiness Benedict XVI, December 24, 2005, at the Vatican website.

after more ephemeral prior and posterior effusions have perished. In his homily, the pope, without citing Ephrem directly, picked up on the same theme in describing a piece of episcopal vesture:

> The symbolism of the Pallium is even more concrete: the lamb's wool is meant to represent the lost, sick, or weak sheep which the shepherd places on his shoulders and carries to the waters of life. For the Fathers of the Church, the parable of the lost sheep, which the shepherd seeks in the desert, was an image of the mystery of Christ and the Church. The human race—every one of us—is the sheep lost in the desert which no longer knows the way. The Son of God will not let this happen; he cannot abandon humanity in so wretched a condition. He leaps to his feet and abandons the glory of heaven, in order to go in search of the sheep and pursue it, all the way to the Cross. He takes it upon his shoulders and carries our humanity; he carries us all—he is the good shepherd who lays down his life for the sheep.
>
> What the Pallium indicates first and foremost is that we are all carried by Christ. But at the same time it invites us to carry one another. Hence the Pallium becomes a symbol of the shepherd's mission.... The pastor must be inspired by Christ's holy zeal: for him it is not a matter of indifference that so many people are living in the desert. And there are so many kinds of desert. There is the desert of poverty, the desert of hunger and thirst, the desert of abandonment, of loneliness, of destroyed love. There is the desert of God's darkness, the emptiness of souls no longer aware of their dignity or the goal of human life. The external deserts in the world are growing, because the internal deserts have become so vast. Therefore the earth's treasures no longer serve to build God's garden for all to live in, but they have been made to serve the powers of exploitation and destruction. The Church as a whole and all her Pastors, like Christ, must set out to lead people out of the desert, towards the place of life, towards friendship with the Son of God, towards the One who gives us life, and life in abundance.[3]

---

3   Text from the Vatican website.

How different is this Christ-like shepherd depicted by Benedict XVI from the wicked shepherd discussed by the Prophet Zechariah (11:4–5, 16–17):

> Thus says the Lord my God: Feed the flock of slaughter, whose possessors slay them and hold themselves not guilty; and those who sell them say, "Blessed be the Lord, for I am rich." And their own shepherds do not pity them.

Here, then, is a shepherd who lets his human sheep be slain by mortal sin and holds himself unresponsible for their slaughter; who sells them off and does not regret their loss to the hands of strangers; who has no pity for the lost and straying, the wretched and impoverished. Strikingly, Zechariah even prophesies that God will "raise up" such a shepherd (in the language of Scripture, this means He will permit it to happen):

> I will raise up a shepherd in the land who will not visit those who are cut off, nor seek those who are scattered, nor heal that which is broken, nor feed that which stands; but he will eat the flesh of the fat sheep and will tear their hooves in pieces. Woe to the worthless shepherd who leaves the flock! The sword shall be upon his arm and upon his right eye. His arm shall be clean dried up, and his right eye shall be utterly darkened.

Every prophet in the Bible says the same. For example, Ezekiel:

> Son of man, prophesy against the shepherds of Israel, prophesy, and say unto them, even to the shepherds, Thus saith the Lord Jehovah: Woe unto the shepherds of Israel that do feed themselves! should not the shepherds feed the sheep? Ye eat the fat, and ye clothe you with the wool, ye kill the fatlings; but ye feed not the sheep.... And they were scattered, because there was no shepherd; and they became food to all the beasts of the field, and were scattered.... Behold, I am against the shepherds; and I will require my sheep at their hand, and cause them to cease from feeding the sheep; neither shall the shepherds feed themselves any more; and I will deliver my sheep from their mouth, that they may not be food for them. (Ezek. 34:2–3, 5, 10)

This shows how important it is to the Lord Jesus Christ, the true Shepherd of Israel, the Ruler of the Church, that His earthly representatives be holy and dutiful in their shepherding, lest they be arraigned for awful judgment on the last day: "Woe to the worthless shepherd who leaves the flock"!

O Lord Jesus Christ,
exemplary servant of the servants of God,
true deacon of mankind!
    You have come to our aid,
time after time, age after age,
in crisis after crisis.
    We beseech you,
hear us and have mercy,
come to our aid even now,
do not delay: deliver us with your strong right arm!
    O Word, penetrating and pervasive
even when derided or ignored:
overcome the cacophony that surrounds us,
restore the wisdom we have squandered in our empty pursuits.
    O Thunder, enter among us and still us before you.
    O Shepherd of Israel, you who lead Joseph like a flock,
Lamb standing as one slain,
redeem us with your precious blood,
and lead us out of the desert
into a land flowing with milk and honey, truth and love.
    Save us, we implore you, from all worthless shepherds,
and bestow on us shepherds after your own Heart.
    Amen.

17

No Matter How Bad You Think the Corruption Is, It's Worse

THE HEART OF THE CURRENT APOSTASY unfolding in the Catholic Church may be stated thus: the Bride of Christ has forsaken her Bridegroom for another lover, the World. Of course, the Bride of Christ in her *perfection,* the Church Triumphant in heaven, can never be unfaithful, nor can the souls already saved but in need of purification, the Church Suffering in purgatory. We are speaking of the Church Militant on earth—and not, obviously, all Catholics, but far too many, especially in the hierarchy. We can see this in an unrelenting flood of bad news that hovers around bishops and cardinals.

We see the abandonment of Christ for the World in the sex abuse scandal surrounding Cardinal McCarrick, predator extraordinaire, and in the ranks of senior clergy who knew about his sinful behavior but refused to do anything about it, even joining in with his hypocrisy. The reaction to the stunning disclosures has been underwhelming, which supports the inference that the McCarrick problem is just the tip of the iceberg.

We see it in the episcopal non-reaction to the fifteen "Catholic" senators who refused to vote against late-term abortions that inflict horrible pain on babies before depriving them of life. Senator Schumer of New York high-fived the "Catholic" senator from North Dakota, rejoicing that the slaughter will continue. Satan smiled on that one. Silence from the bishops. You can bet that if those fifteen senators voted against a "comprehensive immigration reform" bill, the bishops would have immediately called them on the carpet for their cruelty towards the poor.

We see it in Cardinal Cupich's warm welcome to Fr. James Martin, bridge-builder for sins that cry out to heaven for vengeance, and in his hatred for the Church's liturgical tradition, which overflows into enmity against the Canons Regular of St. John Cantius.

We see it in the support given by the same Cupich, together with Archbishop Gregory, Bishop McElroy, and Bishop Wester, to the openly heretical "Association of United States Catholic Priests" (AUSCP), based in Cleveland, Ohio—a clerical version of Call to Action. In any normal situation, all the members of this association and its patrons would have been excommunicated and told to do penance on bread and water until reconciliation might be possible.

We see it in the utter lack of seriousness with which the bishops and clergy of Ireland prepared their people for the fateful referendum on abortion, as a result of which, for the first time ever, a nation democratically turned against the unborn and declared open hunting season on its own children. Efforts to speak the truth in love and unmask the abortionist propaganda were almost solely the work of laity supported with private funds.

We see it in the Vatican "deal" with Communist China, by which the persecuted faithful children of the Church have been betrayed. (Interesting how nobody who lives under Communism ever favors such rapprochements—just the Communist agents in the clergy, like Bishop Sorondo, who said "Right now, those who are best implementing the social doctrine of the Church are the Chinese.")

We see it in Cardinal Marx and his allies, who receive no rebuke when they violate all that is most sacred, giving the Holy Eucharist to adulterers and non-Catholics, plundering monasteries for their property, and pushing forward the schism of the modernist "synodal way." Meanwhile, the good and faithful servant Cardinal Sarah is swiftly rebuked if he dares to recommend the celebration of Mass *ad orientem*—a practice all Catholics had followed for nearly 2,000 years, and one that has, in any case, always been permissible with the new liturgical books.

Alas, one could go on and on. The deafening silence of many among our shepherds, their complicity with evil, their outright espousal of errors, is the great burden we are being asked to bear today in the Church. It is quite like the situation in Henry VIII's England, when most of the bishops were cowards who went along with the new order and the holders of power. St. John Fisher stood out, almost alone, for his unyielding fidelity.

As Pope Paul VI recognized in his famous homily on June 29, 1972, "from some fissure the smoke of Satan has entered the temple of God." The Devil has indeed infiltrated the Church and has recruited many useful idiots and fellow-travelers. Souls are being lost every day because they are led astray by worldly shepherds, wolves in sheep's clothing.

In the sixteenth century, a nun in Quito, Ecuador, Mariana Francisca de Jésus Torres y Berriochoa, received visions of Our Lady of Good Success, subsequently approved by the Church, in which the Holy Mother of God spoke many prophesies of future times. This one in particular stands out:

> During this unfortunate epoch, injustice will even enter here [into the Church], my closed garden. Disguised under the name of false charity, it will wreak havoc in souls. The spiteful demon will try to sow discord, making use of putrid members, who, masked by the appearance of virtue, will be like decaying sepulchers emanating the pestilence of putrefaction, causing moral deaths in some and lukewarmness in others.... How the Church will suffer on that occasion the dark night of the lack of a Prelate and Father to watch over them with paternal love, gentleness, strength, and prudence!

Can any honest Catholic deny that we are living through the exact times of which Our Lady of Good Success warned us? Yet we know, when everything looks its bleakest and all human solutions have fallen away, that her Immaculate Heart will triumph.

We are living through a great purification. To St. Augustine is attributed the remark that the saints of the end times will have no further purging to endure after their life, since they will have already gone through it in this world. We must remain steadfast, weathering the storm, for Christ is still in the boat, silent though He may be, and it will never sink as long as He is near us and we are near Him.

Most commentators do not begin to understand the true nature of the problem.[1]

The ring of criminal Nancy Boys is the same ring that has been sedulously working for decades to undermine the integrity

---

1 The substance of the following paragraphs derives from correspondence with a long-time observer of the modern ecclesiastical scene, who gave me his permission to make use of it.

of the doctrinal, moral, sacramental, liturgical Church. These men—McCarrick, McElroy, Wuerl, O'Malley, Mahony, Cupich, Tobin, Farrell, Lynch, Weakland, Paglia, Maradiaga, their lovable mouthpiece James Martin, Thomas Rosica, and far too many others, including ones who have passed on to their eternal fate, such as Lyons, Boland, Brom—are the same ones who have destabilized and adulterated catechesis, theology, liturgy, and most obviously the Church's commitment to the unchanging moral law, as we saw in the *Amoris Laetitia* debacle and all that surrounded and succeeded it. We must connect the dots and not pretend to be shocked when we see, for example, attempts under way to "re-interpret" *Humanae Vitae* through a false teaching on conscience, or to do away with clerical celibacy, or to introduce female deacons.

To treat the sins of this ring of conspirators as nothing more than a recrudescence of the sex scandals of the past would be to lose sight of their real enormity. These are not just men of bad moral character; they are apostates who are trying to remake the Church in the image of their own apostasy. The Church has been smashed up in front of our eyes in slow motion for decades and few can even begin to admit that we are now faced with a Church in actual smithereens. The Nancy Boys have conducted their campaign of demolition with a kind of imperial sway. It is not this or that aspect of the Church that is corrupt; the rot is now everywhere. It is a rot on which the McCarrick Ring still sups, like maggots feasting on a corpse. For this reason, to hear well-meaning people say Bergoglio must impanel some investigative body to set things right is Alice in Wonderland lunacy. It's like putting Himmler in charge of Nuremberg.

We do not need bishops engaging in public penance (although it's a good idea for their souls and long overdue); we do not need episcopal investigations; we do not need new procedures and new policies. These are all cries for exculpation. Bishops beating their breasts and then going back to doing nothing about the manifest apostasy at the very heart of the Church will not solve matters. We need the apostates identified, denounced, and removed. We need a reaffirmation of the One, Holy, Catholic, and Apostolic Faith. To clean up this mess, we have to clean up more than the scandal of homosexuality, with all of its attendant horrors. We have to denounce and reject the apostasy that powerful and influential homosexuals and their friends have insinuated into the Church over decades.

Take one example that can stand for many others: Rembert Weakland. The man who paid half a million dollars to a former male partner in litigation, who said sexual abuse reporters were "squealing," who shredded reports about such abuse and claimed in his autobiography that he did not know that abuse of children is a crime—this was the same man who worked against traditional sacred music (chant and polyphony), calling for modern styles and liturgical dancing; who, according to a source living in Rome at the time, induced a hesitating Paul VI to push forward the *Novus Ordo Missae*; who criticized the CDF's document *Dominus Jesus* that reaffirmed Catholic dogma on the necessity of faith in Christ and membership in the Church for salvation; and who utterly devastated the historic cathedral of St. John the Evangelist in Milwaukee with a wreckovation that can only be described as satanic.

It is a package deal. This, above all, is what people need to see. The moral depravity, the doctrinal heresy, the liturgical devastation—all of it goes together. If you have the courage to follow each thread, you will find that any attack on one part of the Church, one aspect of her life, one component of her tradition, already is or will soon be bound up with an attack on the other parts, too. The real "seamless garment" is Catholicism taken in its totality. Either you have the whole or you can't have any of it.

Living the devout life—the life of grace enjoined by Christ—is not a mere "option" for the Catholic faithful, even less for Catholic clergy. Living the devout life is a solemn obligation before Almighty God, before the Church, and before one's own conscience. Those who reject or seek to travesty that life will necessarily fall into apostasy. *All* of us will, not just the homosexuals.

The difference with the clerical sodomites is that they become *professional* apostates. It is not enough for them not to believe in the sacraments; they must make others not believe in them as well. They will not stop twisting and mutilating the Church until she blesses their sin, along with many other sins. To achieve their goals, they must wreak havoc on every last aspect of the Church. This is what the *faithful* must stop—forget about the contemptible bureaucracy of the USCCB with its well-heeled lawyers and slick marketeers. We begin to stop the havoc by calling its source by its real name. McCarrick was not just a predatory sodomite, but an *apostate*, and all of his "brother bishops" who knew about the double life and still got their pictures taken with him, laughing away at the latest wool pulled over the people's eyes—you know, the ones who are putting out videos about how *unfortunate* this is, what a *mess*, and, you know, it isn't as bad as people are making it out to be—these are all apostates, too. They're company men with company cars, driving in a long line to their own burials at the ecumenical cemetery.

One would think the collaborationist bishops would think twice before leaving their bunkers. Yet, as recent tweets, videos, and articles have demonstrated, they are oddly reckless—proof that they underestimate the extent to which their "narratives" (such as they are) no longer persuade or even matter. The tide is turning against the privileged clerical elite and their lavish lavender lifestyles.

One has to marvel at the farcical tenacity of so much denial on so many sides, and the ridiculous lengths to which people will go in the attempt to explain away obvious evils. When did Catholics become so delusive, so resistant to reality, so willing to do anything rather than look at the wreckage staring them in the face? Why do so many of us have a problem with calling a spade a spade? The solution will come only when heads roll, many heads, rolling freely. Let the filth be mucked out, and let fresh air and sunlight in.

The Catholic Church is being rocked to its foundations by a Modernist apostasy of staggering proportions. We are in "$2 + 2 = 5$" territory, and the "conservative" apologists have no real response to that, which is why they insist on treating the McCarrick business as a sex scandal. They are more concerned about a mendacious, ramshackle, unaccountable episcopate than they are about the deposit of the faith under daily assault, as it has been ever since the progressive European bishops maneuvered into control of the Second Vatican Council, strewing ambiguities and half-truths in its documents and dominating its implementation, particularly in the liturgical sphere—all of which has led us straight into the cesspool of iniquity and heresy in which we are stewing.

We have a colossal problem on our hands, yes, but it is not insurmountable. The above analysis may seem hopeless, but I am not one of those who believe that ecclesial doom is just around the corner. The papacy can be set right with a worthy pope. The episcopacy can be strengthened if that worthy pope takes action to depose and defrock bishops across the globe and replace them with men worthy of their offices. The seminaries can be reformed. The Mass of Ages can be restored. Catholic education can be revived. Catechesis can be regenerated (but not, needless to say, with the latest version of the *Catechism*).

You may well say: All this, any of this, would be a miracle, heaps of miracles! And I say: Yes, that's right. Miracles do happen, and we need them now more than ever. With man, it is impossible; with God, nothing is impossible—not even the reform of the papacy, the episcopacy, and the college of cardinals.

Reform begins where it always does in the history of the Church through the ages: with faithful laity, faithful priests and deacons, faithful religious brothers and sisters, faithful bishops—men and women absolutely committed to Our Lord and to the Catholic Faith He has given us, in all of its doctrinal integrity, moral strength, and liturgical fullness.

I want to be part of the solution, not part of the problem—and so should you, and every layman, religious, and cleric whom God in His Providence has put into the world at exactly *this* time, so that we can be part of the solution. No one needs to strut off into permanent opposition or lock down in motionless despondency. It is time to pray for divine intervention like never before, and then to work with all our strength and skill to make ready the coming of the Lord.

18

Our Spiritual Response
to Scandals and Abuses

THERE'S NO USE DENYING IT OR PRETEND-
ing otherwise: all Catholics who are clued in to what's
happening are in a state of shock. We opened a plain
door marked "McCarrick" and found on the other side of it a
veritable industry of corruption. The pope's deafening silence in
the face of serious evidence of complicity only rubs salt in the
raw wounds of the People of God.

I have felt sick with grief, disgust, and anger. The arrogance
of the wicked, who strut and boast, who lie and expect Catholics
to swallow their lies like vitamins for good children, is enough
to enrage—or, if one's temperament is less choleric, to induce a
deep depression. Those who found words with which to articulate
a response have poured forth a nearly endless stream of articles
and appeals, all of which fall on deaf ears, or elicit tone-deaf
responses from cardinals in windy cities who, apparently clueless
about how their words will sound to laity already fed up with
bureaucratic evasion, talk about racism, ecology, clericalism, and
other supposedly "more important things."

Feelings of sorrow, abhorrence, bitterness, anger, melancholy—
these feelings are good and right to have at a time like this, since
they are part of the natural "equipment" God has given us for
reacting to present evils, threatening evils, or good things taken
away. But emotions are meant to lead us somewhere, to open up
a path forward, so that we can get beyond the emotion into a
stronger spiritual state and appropriate action. These emotions,
while right and understandable in themselves, are not ends to
rest in, but openings to a new realization and a new resolution.

"It is good to confide in the Lord rather than to have confidence
in man. It is good to trust in the Lord, rather than to trust in
princes" (Ps. 117:8–9)—yea, even princes of the Church. "Blessed
is the man whose trust is in the name of the Lord; and who hath
not had regard to vanities, and lying follies" (Ps. 39:5). "Praise the

Lord, O my soul, in my life I will praise the Lord: I will sing to my God as long as I shall be. Put not your trust in princes: in the children of men, in whom there is no salvation" (Ps. 145:2–3).

Could the message of the Word of God be any clearer? The Church of Christ is founded on the apostles and built on the rock of Peter, absolutely; but this one, holy, catholic, and apostolic Church transmits the orthodox faith and confers on us the grace of the sacraments *through* her ministers, not *from* them; they are not the authors but the dispensers. Their words and works, too, are measured against an unbending measure of truth. The clergy have no special access to this truth, nor to the grace in which we stand. Our Lord who is "full of grace and truth," and all the means of salvation He has given us, are the common good, the united possession, of all believers. To think otherwise would be clericalism indeed.

Our Lord says to each of us: "I the Lord have called you in righteousness; I will take you by the hand and keep you" (Is. 42:6). "I will never fail you nor forsake you" (Heb. 13:5; cf. Josh. 1:5). If there is one thing we know from Scripture and the lives of the saints, it is that the Lord is near to the brokenhearted, and the crushed in spirit He will save (Ps. 33:19). "I will make darkness light before them, and crooked places straight. These things will I do, and I will not forsake them" (Is. 42:16).

And what is our response to this gracious gift of the Lord's call, His unfailing love, His nearness, and His promise to save? "Here is a call for the endurance of the saints, those who keep the commandments of God and the faith of Jesus" (Rev. 14:12). What does the endurance of the saints consist in? Above all, prayer. Nothing can defeat a man or a woman of prayer. Moreover, the devil cannot pray, and the one thing he hates the most is our prayer. When we pray, we are heaping burning coals upon him and all who are in league with him. So the most important thing we must do now is pray: increase our attendance and devotion at Mass; increase our Eucharistic adoration; increase our commitment to the Rosary; increase our use of confession; increase our penances. Some demons, Our Lord assures us, are not driven out except through prayer and fasting (cf. Mt. 17:21).

Our primary work is to stay close to Jesus, using the tried and true means He has given us in His Church from ages past, from the example of the saints, from the wisdom of Scripture and Tradition. That has always been and will always be the main "engine" of ecclesial reform. This is a time for heroic faith, steely hope, and fiery love, as we cry out to our Redeemer: "Arise, O Lord, help us and redeem us for Thy Name's sake" (Ps. 43:26).

In the midst of the current second tidal wave of clerical sex abuse allegations and revelations—a wave likely to continue building in magnitude as it sweeps through one diocese after another and churns up decades of episcopally-authorized muck—we have to guard against and help others to guard against certain popular errors that always crop up at a time like this.

Years ago, I remember reading seven or eight letters to the editor in an old issue of *Time* magazine, an issue with an oil-covered seabird on the cover. These were letters written in reaction to the hierarchy's complicity with clerical abuse, about which we are rightfully indignant. Almost all of the letters reflected the liberal stance of *Time* itself, and all of them revealed a level of ignorance of basic Catholic doctrine that could only be called stupendous.

One fellow's argument boiled down to this: "The Church claims to speak for Christ on earth and so to be infallible, but when the sins of the clergy are exposed, the Church says she is made up of fallible sinners. Which will it be?" How about we make some distinctions?

Another lady wrote: "If my pope doesn't clean up the abuse crisis, I will gladly join all those who are leaving the Church." So, the pope is personally responsible for all sins, and if he doesn't magically put an end to them, one should leave?

Another fellow wrote that he believes in Catholic doctrine but totally rejects the authority of the pope and the hierarchy. That's a head-scratcher. And on and on it goes.

Often at these times we also hear about people tempted to "go East" and become Orthodox. As if this would help one bit! While we may and should admire the liturgical traditions and mystical heritage of the Orthodox, they are as much of a disaster in the arenas of doctrine and morals as Roman Catholics are today, if not worse—and they don't have the benefit of enjoying good popes from time to time. Faithful Catholics claim that *Amoris Laetitia* is a big problem because parts of it contradict the Gospel, and that permissiveness regarding contraception, contrary to the teaching of *Humanae Vitae*, is one step on the road to abortion; but these are the sort of contradictions under which the Orthodox have been laboring for centuries.

What do these sorts of reactions among Catholics show? First of all, they show that the faith is not being taught and preached. No one knows it; what is worse, no one knows that he doesn't know it. It is the blind leading the blind. A Mormon toddler knows more about Joseph Smith's fanciful golden tablets than your average adult Catholic knows about the Blessed Sacrament or Church teaching on marriage and family. It demonstrates that many bishops and pastors have been and continue to be sleeping at the wheel and have hardly begun to assess the true magnitude of the post-conciliar collapse. It is evident that catechesis is still in a state of dire inadequacy, indeed utter vacuity.

We might start with explaining in what the Church's infallibility (and therefore the pope's) actually consists, and in what it does not; the distinction between a man's holy office, which deserves respect, and his individual person, which may or may not be worthy of that office, and can be deserving of reproach, rebuke, and punishment; the difference between obedience and its counterfeits.[1] We should clarify why the Catholic Church and her sacraments are necessary for salvation, and that it is *Christ* in whom we believe, Christ who sanctifies us and saves us. And we should not ignore the terribly pressing urgency of cleaning up our own house, beginning with the sacred liturgy. For the crisis through which the Church is now passing parallels the replacement of the traditional Mass and the other sacraments, thick and rich and full of religion, with modern "low fat" versions that have failed to nourish and have lent themselves to every type of willfulness, banality, and abuse.

Moreover, these reactions show the extent of the damage that Catholics have suffered in these decades, the pain and righteous indignation they feel, and the legitimate demands for justice they put forward. Ultimately, the only ones who can right the institutional wrongs are the members of the hierarchy itself. Lay people can investigate and accuse and even prosecute, but the systemic abuse of ecclesiastical authority will be counteracted and conquered only from the top down. We currently have a largely

---

1   For a full treatment of this subject, see my tract *True Obedience in the Church*.

dysfunctional institution and it does no good to pretend otherwise. Admitting the truth is the beginning of the reform.

Abandoning the Church in her hour of need is the very worst thing any believer can do. In fact, it is exactly what the devil is looking for: people who throw out the baby with the bathwater, who lose sight of Jesus Christ and His plan for the Church, getting bogged down in the Antichrist and His counterplan for the Church. It is at just such a time of crisis that opportunities for heroic faith, prayer, sacrifice, and zeal multiply and bear the most fruit.

We have grown accustomed to a world of media that spins and distorts everything it handles, indulges at whim in suppression or falsification of truth, and pushes its own agendas without the slightest qualms of conscience. We are reeling from many indications that the world of the Catholic hierarchy *also* spins, distorts, suppresses, and falsifies while driving forward the liberal agenda. In the midst of such a hostile environment, all Catholics— and most of all, the bishops and cardinals who *are* faithful to Christ and His Church—must take to heart the words of Saint Paul:

> I charge you in the presence of God and of Christ Jesus who is to judge the living and the dead, and by his appearing and his kingdom: preach the word, be urgent in season and out of season, convince, rebuke, and exhort, be unfailing in patience and in teaching. (2 Tim. 4:1-2)

"IT IS IMPOSSIBLE THAT SCANDALS SHOULD NOT come: but woe to him through whom they come" (Lk. 17:1). "In the world you shall have distress: but have confidence, I have overcome the world" (Jn. 16:33).

In recent months, nothing has been more talked about in connection with the Catholic Church than that bitter, unspeakably sad two-syllable word, *scandal*. It is almost as if the world, the flesh, and the devil, of whom the secular media are the ready mouthpiece, were rejoicing in full choir that they have been able to draw the attention of so many people away from Christ our King, victorious upon the Cross, exalted at the right hand of the Father, towards the muddy depths of human weakness and sin—including not only the reeking sins of lower clergy but also the sins of ambition, mendacity, and cowardice on the part of bishops.

Contrary to what some popes may say on their bad days, we should not be ignoring accusations of episcopal evil as if they were from the devil.[2] Too many chancery offices have tried the approach of whistling in the dark and pretending that nothing's really the matter, which is just as unchristian as frolicking in the mud of calumny or detraction.

I believe, however, that we must look at the evils around us and within us *peripherally,* in the light of the Cross. Our Lord Jesus Christ alone can give us the strength to face evils of this magnitude and overcome them. In His truth we see our sins; in His love we see our liberation; in His grace we find our constant help. He is the only one who can bring any of us to true repentance for our sins and make us whole again. This, then, is how we know we are dealing with scandals in a Christian way: when we think to pray for a bishop's or cardinal's repentance and salvation, in addition to demanding that justice be done in the Church.

Here is something that needs to be said to all Christians, especially those whose faith is wavering on account of scandals: the fundamental miracle or miraculousness of the Catholic Church is not her *perfection,* but her *existence.*

It is true that Holy Mother Church shows us countless models of supreme holiness in the saints, but they are revelations of what the Church is called and guaranteed to be in her final state, not a democratic cross-section of what she actually is. What is astonishing is the fact that such a thing as the Church even *exists* in the fallen world—a spiritual temple in which God's eternal life is shared with man, where God is made truly ours by sanctifying grace, where the Lamb of God is fed to us in the Eucharist. In this, there is cause enough for a hundred or a thousand lifetimes of wonder. Evil tarnishes and diminishes the Church in our midst, but it can never obliterate the miracle of her existence or make the gifts she offers to mankind any less wondrous and glorious than they are.

"No man has ever spoken as this man has spoken," the Gospel says of Jesus (Jn. 7:46). I have often said to my students, I am a Christian because I am in love with Jesus Christ, "the Son of God, who loved me and gave himself for me" (Gal. 2:20); and I

---

2   A reference to Pope Francis's repeated claims in 2018 and 2019 that those who attempt to expose clerical corruption are doing the work of the devil, the "great accuser."

am Roman Catholic because there is no other way of being sure to possess Jesus as the Way, the Truth, and the Life except by belonging to the community He founded, making use of all the means of salvation He entrusted to it.[3]

Hence, when I see the sins within me, and I see the corruption around me, even all the way to the top of the Church's hierarchy, I say with Simon Peter: "Lord, to whom shall we go? *You* have the words of eternal life" (Jn. 6:68). No one can change those words of His, nor the promise He backs up with His death and resurrection, nor the grace He gives to the brokenhearted. This is what brings me peace and joy, if I only pause for a moment and call to mind what Jesus has done and is doing for me and for so many others who strive to follow Him.

Only if I become a saint will I make a difference to anyone else inside or outside the Church; and the only way to become a saint is to become one with Jesus on the Cross. We stand beneath the Cross with Mary and John, at the bleakest moment, when all hope seems lost, when Christ is dying in agony and gives up his last breath, and the storm hits. Even after the resurrection, the Church sojourning in time never leaves the foot of the Cross. The bride has to suffer *all* that her bridegroom suffered, if she is to share fully in the victory He has won.

---

3   See "A Reply to the Discouraged Seminarian: There Are 6,000 Reasons to Remain Catholic," *OnePeterFive*, May 20, 2021.

19

Why Remain Catholic,
in Spite of Everything

DEAR DR. KWASNIEWSKI,

The question that all of Viganò's essays and your own raises is: Why at this point should we remain in communion with the Catholic Church—you know, the one that most people (reasonably?) think is headed by Pope Francis and the bishops in communion with him? If Vatican II was faulty and the popes from John XXIII on have all been Modernists in varying degrees, as you and others convincingly argue; if full-blooded true Catholicism is found elsewhere than in unity with what was, by all accounts, an ecumenical council and the putative popes who have uncritically endorsed it; then why would any right-thinking believer remain in communion with *that* entity? Why should we rely on councils and popes of said Church if they have manifestly led millions of souls astray? Adopting Viganò's logic and your own, I see no reason to remain in communion with "the Catholic Church" as people today commonly consider it. Can you give me one that is logical?[1]

MY RESPONSE:

"Scio cui credidi..." "I know in whom I have believed" (2 Tim. 1:12), as the Introit reminds us on the feast of St. Paul's Conversion. Faith is a gift from God: "It is not you who have

---

1   A letter sent to me by a reader. It seems appropriate, at this first mention of the name of the controversial Archbishop Carlo Maria Viganò, to explain briefly my stance toward him and his work. I consider his stunning documents on the McCarrick affair to be a momentous "house-cleaning" intervention for which he has been vindicated and will be lauded in the annals of Church history. I found myself in agreement with much else that he wrote between 2018 and early 2021, as collected in the volume *A Voice in the Wilderness*, ed. Brian M. McCall (Brooklyn, NY: Angelico Press, 2021), and I gladly included his response to *Traditionis Custodes* in the volume *From Benedict's Peace to Francis's War*. However, I absolutely part ways with the archbishop's views on Vladimir Putin and the Russian war against Ukraine.

chosen me but I who have chosen you," says the Lord (Jn. 15:16). This faith is directed to the Trinity and the Incarnation, and then to the Church and her "system" as an extension and continuation of these fundamental mysteries. For me, being Catholic is about embracing these mysteries, holding fast to Jesus Christ, especially in the act of worship and communion. The Church is where He lives and dwells, and where I am joined with Him.

The sacred liturgy is, for me, not just theoretically but quite practically the font and apex (*fons et culmen*) of my life as a Catholic—and by this, I mean the traditional liturgy, since I can no longer recognize in the Novus Ordo a legitimate liturgical rite of the Roman Church, even if it is sacramentally valid and may serve a temporary purpose, as a rickety life raft aids the shipwrecked until they can be rescued by a proper boat. As Martin Mosebach says: "The liturgy IS the Church—every Mass celebrated in the traditional spirit is immeasurably more important than every word of every pope. It is the red thread that must be drawn through the glory and misery of Church history; where it continues, phases of arbitrary papal rule will become footnotes of history."[2]

As the foregoing already suggests, I am not one of those who assumes that the Church is to be equated with popes, bishops, and councils. They obviously play a role in articulating the content of the deposit of faith and condemning errors that threaten her members, but it is a supporting role, not the star of the show. Our hierarchs can also fail in their responsibilities, as we can see plainly whether we cast our eyes over the pages of ecclesiastical history or simply look around us today. God mercifully provides us with many means of knowing the truth and adhering to it, even when the shepherds of the Church turn into wolves. In the best of times, we can and should trust the shepherds, but at the worst of times, such as ours, their dereliction or apostasy becomes apparent and undeniable. Then, we do not trust them or follow them, unless we want to perish in the destruction God has promised to visit upon hypocrites, heretics, idolaters, and sodomites (to mention the most relevant categories).

Most of what we believe as Catholics—the *substance of our faith*—has already been solemnly defined or universally taught for centuries,

---

2   *The Heresy of Formlessness: The Roman Liturgy and Its Enemy*, trans. Graham Harrison (Brooklyn, NY: Angelico Press, 2018), 188.

so there's not much a pope (or a council, for that matter) could add or change. I cannot think of a single doctrine of any significance that has not already been "nailed down" by now, or the opposite of which has not been anathematized. This fact could be demonstrated, were any demonstration needed, by a cursory review of hundreds of catechisms published with ecclesiastical approbation over the span of the last five centuries. Here we see the monumental stability of the Church's teaching, consistent from one end of the world to the other. For most people, the *Catechism of Trent*, the *Baltimore Catechism*, or the *Catechism of Pius X* would be more than sufficient for acquiring the mind of the Church in her universal ordinary Magisterium.

Now, someone might rejoinder: "Isn't the papacy and its prerogatives part of that immutable catechetical content?" Of course it is—but according to the realistic and limited understanding of the papacy that was given expression in the First Vatican Council. A Catholic no more rejects the papal office than he expects to find a mammal without a head; yet neither does he think of the head as if it were monstrously outsized for the body, or the only place where the soul of the Mystical Body, the Holy Spirit, dwells. The pope, like the least layman, has to function *within* the body according to the role he has received from Divine Providence; the pope, like the lowliest sinner, can deviate from the path of truth in all but his most solemn acts of pontifical definition, when he is guaranteed the assistance of the Holy Spirit. I recall reading in Fr. Garrigou-Lagrange a penetrating sentence about the motives for belief in Christianity. It went something like this: "There is light enough for those who wish to believe, and obscurity enough for those who wish not to believe." Similarly, we might say about the papacy that historical instances of serious deviation have been rare enough to confirm our faith in the divine support of the papal office, yet numerous enough to warn us against a submission unenlightened by the Catholic Faith and the exercise of reason.

Here I think it is high time to clear up an all-too-common misconception, namely, that traditionalists are anti-authoritarians and individualists. Nothing could be further from the truth. A traditionalist *wants* the guidance of the Magisterium—he is not looking to go off Protestant-like into his own sect. He *wants* to be able to follow the pope, the diocesan bishop, and the local pastor; He would much prefer assenting to and absorbing all that they teach. By the very inclination of grace, he wishes to be a member of the body, a part of the whole, a citizen of the celestial commonwealth; individualism is abhorrent.

The trouble starts when the so-called "living Magisterium" seems plainly to be contradicting or muddying the longstanding Magisterium notable for its consistency and clarity, or when disciplinary decisions, so far from honoring and strengthening Catholic practice, take the modern "cancel culture" approach. Such problems are not matters of arcane discernment, requiring gnostic access to hidden wisdom. They stand up and hit you in the face; they bruise faith and batter reason. At that point, what are we to do? Do we just assume that everyone before us was wrong, and that Christianity consists in an evolutionary process with no fixed nature and no definite goal, except perhaps a space-age Omega Point? No, we don't assume that, unless we wish to barter away our baptism in Christ Jesus, "the same yesterday, today, and forever" (Heb. 13:8), and unless we wish to cease "contending earnestly for the faith once delivered to the saints" (Jude 3). We hold on to that which is certain, and we question that which is strange or novel against the backdrop of our inherited liturgy, doctrine, and morals (*lex orandi, lex credendi, lex vivendi*).

Do we have to be brilliant theologians? No. It is enough for a traditionally catechized Catholic to refuse to assent to or live by anything that savors or smells of novelty, heresy, impiety, immorality. We might be mistaken in our judgment of this or that particular matter, but that's hardly a problem, since we can never go wrong by holding to what is known with certainty and confidence, and by following the teaching and example of the great saints of the past, who lived by the same Catholic Faith. It is not up to the sheep to twist themselves into pretzels in order to accommodate modernist teaching; rather, it is up to the shepherds to speak the language of Catholicism.

If Christianity is true, the only serious contenders for its earthly representative are the Catholic Church and the Eastern Orthodox (in all their ethno-national variety). While I admire the Eastern liturgy and cherish Eastern Christian spiritual writers, my study of Eastern theology and history leaves me less impressed. In order to become Orthodox, I would have to expressly renounce the *Filioque*, the Immaculate Conception, Purgatory, and the infallibility of the pope in *ex cathedra* pronouncements. I could not do this, since all of these doctrines make sense to me. That they make sense to me is not (I hasten to add) the reason why I *accept* them; my point is that even my reason sees enough of their profound harmony with the rest of revealed truth that I could not reject them without being irrational.

What we are seeing from the Vatican is a sort of bizarre game in which they hem and haw, ignore doctrines, invent new formulations, and in general try to obfuscate what our tradition has illuminated and clarified. From Vatican II onwards, modern churchmen have consistently *refused* to exercise their authority to the full, preferring to sermonize endlessly in support of their favorite causes. I'm not denying that at some level the Magisterium has been and is being "engaged," but it is at a level compatible with error or just plain stupidity and unhelpful vagueness. The only really important judgments that have been made concern sexual and bioethical issues. Apart from that, there is almost nothing from the past sixty years that will go down in history as a "high point" for the Church. Our era bears more resemblance to the Dark Ages, with its centuries of civil and ecclesiastical corruption, influx of non-Christian and anti-Christian peoples, and spotty transmission of heritage by a few literate people.

And yet, the parallels extend only so far. I see no way around the conclusion that we are living in an unprecedented era. Modernity—by which I mean not just a chronological period but a philosophical and anthropological outlook—is more disoriented and degenerate than any phase that has ever occurred in human history, and the crisis in the Church mirrors this uniqueness in depth and breadth. The *mysterium iniquitatis* is never far away from fallen human beings (and that applies to the Byzantine court no less than to the papal court; rather the contrary). But our current level of chaos and confusion, which has evolved into a studied program, is something new; I would go so far as to call it apocalyptic.

I see the "neo-Magisterium"—that is, conciliar and papal teaching and legislation, to the extent that it departs from hitherto received tradition—as a cancerous growth or tumor in the body of Christ on earth. I do not know when or how the divine Physician will excise it or dissolve it. All I can do is to remain faithful to the Deposit of Faith and its time-honored theological exposition, as it has been given to me to understand it. My conscience bids me to be and to remain a Catholic, so I persevere and suffer, and strive to be a saint in the only way that makes sense: by the old pattern. It is like what we see in religious communities: in the 1960s and 1970s, most of them abandoned their old habits for new ones, then often gave up any habits, and now these orders have died out. The flourishing new communities have resumed the old habits, and the more traditional their vision is, the more they have flourished.

As John Henry Newman once said in regard to the Arian crisis, the teaching office of the bishops appears to be "in suspension": it exists, but the faith is being held and transmitted more by the laity and by the lower clergy than by the hierarchy. I do not see how this shakes the foundations of the Church. What it shakes, rather, is overconfidence in mortal men and princes (cf. Ps. 145:2–3).

The Bride of Christ on earth is one whose visage has been marred by the sins of her members, especially of her most prominent members. But I love the Bride nonetheless, recognizing that it is in *her heavenly glory* that her full essence is found and her full beauty unveiled. The Church on earth is a passing reality; the Church in heaven is what abides. "Communion with the Church" is first and foremost communion with the saints and angels in heaven, and, secondarily, with our glorified Lord under the sacramental veils here below. Where these are found, *there* is the Church, regardless of the corruption of some of her members or the deviations caused by their laying aside of the exercise of her priestly, prophetic, and kingly offices. This is the profound truth of Augustine's anti-Donatist polemic: it is not Fr. So-and-so who baptizes, but Christ who baptizes; it is not Fr. So-and-so who confects the Eucharist or whom we receive in it, but Christ Himself. God so loved the world that He did not send a committee. In that way, my faith in Christ and in the means of salvation He has provided remains unshaken; indeed, it has become even stronger in this time of crisis.

As she appears in her present earthly configuration, the Catholic Church has no credibility to the world, for she looks, speaks, and acts like the world: the world has claimed her, to make of her what it wants, to have its way with her. Or rather, those who speak and act on behalf of the Church handed her over to the world, thinking thereby to convince it of her benevolence and desire to raise up the lot of man; but the world merely used and ravaged her, and made her into a limp, toothless ape of the world, or, as some have said, Chaplain to the United Nations. This is the Church that holds events like "The Economy of Francesco."

The Church was betrayed by the progressives of Vatican II, just as Christ was betrayed by Judas; and as Peter denied Christ to protect himself, so the hirelings in the Church have abandoned truth until the world stopped bothering them, indeed until it seemed to agree with them; and thereby the Church became the world's "little pet," the lapdog of Soros and friends.

It is extremely painful to watch this happening, when it seems that, humanly speaking, there is nothing we can do about it. It is like watching, from a high position, two trains running towards each other on the same track, which we know will collide. We can shout; we can close our eyes; we can utter a prayer or a less admirable word; but the trains will collide.

As we see in the Gospels, Jesus Christ stood firm and never changed His uncompromising messianic and divine message. For this, he was persecuted and murdered. Likewise, those in the Church who care not for their own life but only for the life of Christ in His Church, these, too, are persecuted and exiled and "put to death"—usually in the form of marginalization and silence.

Yet such ostracization is not, or need not be, the end of the story, any more than the tomb was the end of Christ's life. Judas, the Pharisees and scribes, Pilate and the Roman soldiers, *none* of them could prevent Christ from rising on the third day, exactly when He chose to rise. They could not prevent His apostles, duly chastened, from evangelizing the earth. They could not prevent His kingdom from taking root here below as it directed souls heavenward. Come what may, this Church will not be eradicated, though its fruit be stripped and its branches hewn off.

Traditional Catholics often hear the comment: "But aren't traditionalists just a tiny minority? Why do you think you matter in the big picture? What difference can you possibly make?"

But how much do numbers really matter to God? In fact, upon consideration of the Bible and of Church history, it looks like He prefers to accomplish great things by means of little things—and the greater the work, the littler the means. "My thoughts are not your thoughts, nor my ways your ways . . . " (Is. 55:8). "The foolish things of the world hath God chosen, that he may confound the wise; and the weak things of the world hath God chosen, that he may confound the strong" (1 Cor. 1:27).

He started the entire human race with one man, Adam, and an original couple, Adam and Eve. When they wrecked their lives and ours, He promised to redeem us by the Woman and by her Seed, that is, by two other individuals.

He started the human race over again, so to speak, with Noah and his immediate family.

He started Israel with Abraham and Sarah, the one a bargainer and bigamist, the other a laughing skeptic. From their son Isaac emerged descendants as numerous as the stars of the sky or the sand of the seashore.

He started the New Israel with twelve men. The first four were fishers. Most were rather unremarkable in worldly terms. One of them betrayed Him and all but one fled. From this unpromising beginning came forth a global spiritual empire.

He rejected 31,700 troops of Gideon, preferring to defeat the armies of Midian by means of three hundred picked men. He wanted to make it clear that the victory was *His* to boast of, not Israel's.

The prophet Elijah was the leader of the resistance movement against the cult of Baal, which had all the political power and numbers on its side.

St. Benedict of Nursia started the greatest monastic movement in the history of the world. According to the old *Catholic Encyclopedia*: "At the beginning of the fourteenth century the order is estimated to have comprised the enormous number of 37,000 monasteries. It had up to that time given to the Church no less than 24 popes, 200 cardinals, 7,000 archbishops, 15,000 bishops, and over 1,500 canonized saints."

Something similar could be said of St. Dominic, St. Francis, and St. Ignatius of Loyola. These *individuals*—not the nameless masses or the world of highfalutin courtiers—are the ones who most of all changed the face of the earth. God chooses one in order to bless many; He leads many back to Him by means of the one. When God wishes to intervene decisively in Church history, He does not search the earth for someone already perfect; He looks for one who is willing to be perfected in the crucible of His love.

St. Benedict had to throw himself into the briars, and St. Francis into the snow, to conquer youthful temptations against chastity; St. Ignatius started off as a vainglorious soldier. What set them apart from the mediocre masses was their seriousness in pursuit of holiness, once they set off on that path.

You and I, too, are supposed to be "important individuals who make a crucial difference." Our job, the only one God has given us, is to become saints, and in so doing, to make a difference in a world gone mad by its loss of God, and in a Church gone rotten from its lukewarm members. We will do this primarily by *prayer*; by the study of the Word of God; by stability in our vocations; and by giving fearless witness whenever and wherever demanded. For some it will involve a more active apostolate; for others, on the contrary, it will mean withdrawing into silence and penance.

On the other hand, Scripture paints a sobering picture of the direction that the majority at any time tend to go in: the majority of Adam's fallen descendants ("wide is the gate, and broad is the way that leadeth to destruction, and many there are who go in thereat," Mt. 7:13); the majority of Israelites; the majority of Christians in the early centuries who fell away under persecution; the majority of Christians who became worldly in this or that period of history; the majority of self-identified Catholics today, whose beliefs and lives differ little or nothing from those of their unbelieving liberal neighbors; the overwhelming majority of the episcopacy throughout the world. Can we detect a pattern? What should be surprising to us is any stretch of time, any privileged place, where we see anything *other* than this pattern.

Scripture also tells us that sin maketh nations miserable (Prov. 13:34), and that he who loveth iniquity hateth his own soul (Ps. 10:6; cf. Prov. 8:36). The Church, too, for her own good, cannot escape this law. For churchmen to shut down public Mass and sacramental reception for months, and then to follow it up with an exponential increase in mandatory Eucharistic profanation—I refer to various policies requiring communion in the hand and forbidding it on the tongue—is like someone taking cyanide and then, for good measure, shooting himself in the head. It *will* get results. Namely: the execution of divine wrath, which will sweep away the excuse of the worldly Church as it swept away the temple and nation of the Jews under the impious kings of Judah and Israel.

Like Elijah, we must remember there are still servants of God who will not bend the knee to Baal. We must persevere in prayer and refuse to consent to the wickedness of Baal's servants, while we await our deliverance from God, whose all-seeing wisdom, cosmic timeline, and methods of involvement are not ours.

We do not know what will come. We may suffer sacramental deprivation for long periods of time. We may be forced to go underground and rely on the few priests—they exist in almost every diocese—who are still animated by reverential fear of the Lord and love for the eternal destiny of His flock. It will not be easy, and we must be ready to forego human respect and the psychological consolation of "acting by the books." The state of emergency is not just a remote theoretical possibility; it is increasingly the only environment in which we live.

The greatest miracle of modern times is not the dancing of the sun at Fatima, as marvelous as that was, but the miracle of a Church that has survived its postconciliar mutilation and malnourishment. To be more precise: the standing miracle is the Lord's preservation and protection of a minority of clergy and faithful who have remained true to, or who are awakening to the truth of, Catholic doctrine and tradition, and who are, in fact, *the Church alive* in orthodox faith, in devotion, in the pursuit of virtue. This is the whole Church in miniature, like a potent seed ready to grow again into a great tree, or a leaven ready to lift the dough.

20

Preparing Now for What the Future May Hold

I N MY ARTICLE "HAVE THERE BEEN WORSE Crises Than This One?,"[1] I explained why I believe the Church is in a crisis second to none in her history—a crisis of unique gravity. The question on the minds of many is this: What might happen next—in the near future, in ten years, in twenty years, in fifty years? What might the Church look like if the "new paradigm" of Bergoglio succeeds? It is a question well worth asking in this "Year of *Amoris Laetitia*" (March 19, 2021 to June 26, 2022).

As I like to say, when Pope Francis was elected, my crystal ball exploded. I am fully aware that Church history includes many surprises, good and bad. I see two probable scenarios, and we must be prepared for either of them.

One scenario would be a kind of replay of the sixteenth century, when the Church was facing the Protestant Revolt. We could have a series of popes who go back and forth, see-saw-like, between orthodoxy and heterodoxy, reform and corruption. In the sixteenth century, worldly or ineffective or clueless popes alternated with strong reformatory characters. Our next conclave might by some prodigious miracle produce a Leo XIV or a Benedict XVII who would tilt things back in a traditional direction; but then the conclave after could produce a Francis II who would, like a new liberal pastor at the local parish, undo much of his predecessor's legacy as quickly as possible; and this tug of war could last for fifty or seventy years. In this case, we have to be ready to take advantage of the good moments and stand strong during the evil ones. If we have been paying attention during the Francis pontificate, we have been well and duly warned.

Some believe that, from a strictly human point of view, a second scenario is more likely: we will have a Francis II, a Francis III, and a Francis IV. They will continue to foster violations of the Ten Commandments, the rejection of established dogmas, and the

1   See chapter 4.

profanation of the liturgy, using the tools of ambiguity, winks and nudges, speeches and documents of minimal authority, committees and conferences, and lower-level appointees who will do the heavy lifting. They will attempt to eradicate the traditional Latin Mass, suspend priests who continue to say it, strangle religious communities that use it, and shut down hitherto flourishing churches and chapels.

In such a case, we will have no choice but to resist all such abuses of authority and work around them, as did our predecessors in the traditional movement from the mid-1960s onward.[2] Stratford Caldecott remarks that the beatitude "Blessed are they that mourn" includes "those who remember the dead, and who remain faithful to tradition."[3] We will refuse to cooperate, as did the Catholics in the fourth century when Arian heretics took over episcopal offices and church buildings. As St. Athanasius famously wrote to his faithful flock under persecution:

> May God console you!... What saddens you...is the fact that others have occupied the churches by violence, while during this time you are on the outside. It is a fact that they have the premises—but you have the apostolic Faith. They can occupy our churches, but they are outside the true Faith. You remain outside the places of worship, but the Faith dwells within you. Let us consider: what is more important, the place or the Faith? The true Faith, obviously. Who has lost and who has won in this struggle—the one who keeps the premises or the one who keeps the Faith?
>
> True, the premises are good when the apostolic Faith is preached there; they are holy if everything takes place there in a holy way... You are the ones who are happy: you who remain within the church by your faith, who hold firmly to the foundations of the Faith which has come down to you from apostolic Tradition. And if an execrable jealousy has tried to shake it on a number of

---

2   See Stuart Chessman, *Faith of Our Fathers: A Brief History of Catholic Traditionalism in the United States, from* Triumph *to* Traditionis Custodes (Brooklyn: Angelico Press, 2022).

3   Stratford Caldecott, *Not as the World Gives: The Way of Creative Justice* (Kettering, OH: Angelico Press, 2014), 13.

occasions, it has not succeeded. They are the ones who have broken away from it in the present crisis.

No one, ever, will prevail against your faith, beloved brothers. And we believe that God will give us our churches back some day.

Thus, the more violently they try to occupy the places of worship, the more they separate themselves from the Church. They claim that they represent the Church; but in reality, they are the ones who are expelling themselves from it and going astray.[4]

We may have to go into hiding, as the early Christians were sometimes forced to do, or as English Catholics did under Queen Elizabeth. We will welcome fugitive priests into our homes. Masses will be offered once again in living rooms, basements, attics, hotels, under tents, in forests, open fields, and caves. To this end, I recommend that families build an altar for home use and, if they have room for it, create a chapel. Even if no persecution comes to your corner of the world, the chapel will still be valuable as a place dedicated solely to prayer, and a reminder of the need to place Our Lord at the center of our lives.

In the wonderful interview entitled *Christus Vincit*, Bishop Athanasius Schneider talks about his childhood in the Soviet Union, where the Catholics would be without Mass or Confession for months, even as long as a year, because no clandestine priest could reach them. Then a priest would suddenly come, and everyone would go to Confession and Communion, not knowing the next time they would get the chance. He speaks of the many holy men and women in his family who died holy deaths without the sacraments, but full of faith and love.

The same is true in the world today: so many Christians in China and in the Middle East have no access to the sacraments, but they are being deeply sanctified in their life of prayer and their practice of the virtues. Pope Pius XII asked the world to pray to the "King of Martyrs" for the Chinese Catholics in an

---

4   This translation is taken from "Letter of St. Athanasius" (https://sspx. org/en/letter-st-athanasius); for an alternative from the series *Nicene and Post-Nicene Fathers*, see www.documentacatholicaomnia.eu/03d/1819-1893,_ Schaff._Philip,_3_Vol_04_Athanasius,_EN.pdf, pp. 961-62.

indulgenced prayer he promulgated on July 16, 1957.[5] It is a prayer we may find increasingly applicable to ourselves:

> To those who must suffer torment and violence, hunger and fatigue, be Thou the invincible strength sustaining them in their trials and assuring them of the rewards pledged by Thee to those who persevere to the end.
>
> Many, on the other hand, are exposed to moral constraints, which oftentimes prove much more dangerous inasmuch as they are more deceitful; to such, then, be Thou the light to enlighten their mind, so that they may clearly see the straight path of truth; be Thou also to them a source of strength for the support of their will, so that they may triumph in every crisis and never yield to any vacillation or weakness.
>
> Finally, there are those who find it impossible to profess their faith openly, to lead a normal Christian life, to receive the holy sacraments frequently, and to converse familiarly with their spiritual guides. To such, be Thou Thyself a hidden altar, an invisible temple, a plenitude of grace and a fatherly voice, helping and encouraging them, providing a remedy for their aching hearts and filling them with joy and peace.

Sacramental access has been (relatively speaking) so easy for such a long time in the Western world that we have forgotten about the eras in which a certain deprivation was normal. In its entry on "aliturgical days," the old *Catholic Encyclopedia* describes how the holy mysteries, i.e., the Mass or Divine Liturgy inclusive of the consecration of the bread and wine, was, once upon a time, not celebrated every day of the week:

> Although we do not possess much which can be regarded as direct and clear evidence, there is every reason to believe that in early centuries of the Church aliturgical days were numerous both in East and West. In the beginning of things Mass seems to have been said only on Sundays and on the very few festivals then recognized, or

---

5   The indulgence for this prayer was, tellingly, not renewed in the 1968 *Enchiridion Indulgentiarum* and its later editions. See Joseph Shaw, *The Case for Liturgical Restoration* (Brooklyn, NY: Angelico Press, 2019), 263–64.

perhaps on the anniversaries of the martyrs, the bishop himself officiating. To these occasions we have to add certain days of "stations" which seem to have coincided with the Wednesday and Friday fast then kept regularly throughout the Church. Dom Germain Morin has shown that at Capua, in the sixth century, and also in Spain, Mass was celebrated during Lent only on the Wednesday and the Friday. It is probable that a similar rule, but including the Monday also, obtained in England in the days of Bede or even later (see *Revue Benedictine*, 1891, VIII, 529). At Rome we also know that down to the time of Pope Gregory II (715–731), the liturgy was not celebrated on Thursdays.

As Gregory DiPippo notes: "A similar custom prevails to this day in the Ambrosian and Byzantine Rites, the former abstaining from the Eucharistic Sacrifice on all the Fridays in Lent, the latter on all the weekdays."[6] This ancient praxis, which remains alive among Byzantine Catholics, has a fresh application in our times, when many days of the year must be "aliturgical" for Latin-rite Catholics who adhere to the *usus antiquior*, the authentic liturgy of the Church of Rome. On those days, we can pray a "dry Mass" with our missals, make a spiritual communion, and/or pray some part of the Divine Office (e.g., Prime), which is a nourishing feast for the soul. We should try to think of the times when we are deprived of public liturgy or of the reception of sacraments as purgative and preparative periods in which we can cultivate interior longing for Christ, which is the dry kindling needed for a blazing fire.

What did St. Paul mean when he said: "I determined not to know any thing among you, save Jesus Christ, and him crucified" (1 Cor. 2:2)? The Eucharist, as St. Thomas teaches, is *ipse Christus passus*—Christ Himself, as having suffered for our salvation. But all of the sacraments are, in a way, Christ crucified, since they apply to our souls the fruits of His redemptive Passion. The very structure of the Church, purchased with His Blood, is Christ crucified in His mystical members; the principal action of the Church is the renewal of Christ crucified upon the altar; the entire

---

6 "The Raising of Lazarus in the Liturgy of Lent," *New Liturgical Movement*, March 16, 2018.

Christian life is Christ crucified, as we die to self and live for God; heaven itself is nothing other than Christ crucified, reigning and rejoicing in glory with His life-giving wounds, "a Lamb standing as though slain" (Rev. 5:6). Could I only know "Christ Jesus, and Him crucified," everything else worth knowing would grow out of that as from a mustard seed.

It seems that our times are summoning us in a unique way to a participation in the mystery of the Lord's Passion and Death:

> We should take consolation from our irrelevance. God knows what we do, and its importance is not measured in human terms but in those of divine love. We can sing, dance, do penance and what you will, in the full knowledge that the value of our actions is beyond calculation, as long as they belong to Christ. Most of what we say will be a dead footnote in history. It is our child raising and prayer muttering that threaten to make a difference, if not on this earth, then at least in Purgatory or Heaven.... Find your consolations other than in the "human health" of the Church. We are not wrong to be so scandalised by the current management. We just have to take the pain. It's our cross. We have to bear it. Our love is love unknown. And there is nothing particularly new in that.[7]

Cardinal Sarah, Cardinal Burke, Bishop Schneider—men who preach the same doctrine as their Master, with the calm, credible, and instantly recognizable authority of Successors of the Apostles—have frequently reminded us that we cannot endure and overcome evils of the magnitude we are now seeing in the world and in the Church except by striving to be saints, the "just men" of Abraham's bargain with the Lord (see Gen. 18:16–33). During the Arian controversy, St. Hilary of Poitiers, one of a very few unequivocally Catholic bishops at the time, wrote: "In this consists the particular nature of the Church: that she triumphs when she is defeated, that she is better understood when attacked, that she rises up when her unfaithful members desert her."

As for those unfaithful members, their "getting away with murder" does not have to be our paralysis. We are assured in Scripture, again

---

7   Written years ago by a blogger, "The Sensible Bond," who subsequently left the internet and took down his writings. I have saved some of them.

and again, that the Lord will take care of them—either bringing about their conversion or punishing their wickedness. The words of the Psalmist ring out:

> O Lord, how long shall the wicked,
> how long shall the wicked triumph?
> They prate, they speak arrogantly:
> all the workers of iniquity boast themselves.
> They break in pieces thy people, O Lord,
> and afflict thy heritage ....
> The Lord will not cast off his people,
> neither will he forsake his inheritance.
> For judgment shall return unto righteousness;
> and all the upright in heart shall follow it ....
> Shall the throne of wickedness have fellowship with thee,
> which frameth mischief by statute? ...
> He hath brought upon them their own iniquity,
> and will cut them off in their own wickedness;
> the Lord our God will cut them off.[8]

We do not have to run the universe (thank God!). Our job is to pray for deliverance, for perseverance, for a love that never dies. Our daily exercise is to let go of anger, bitterness, impatience, and despondency, to push it away with a holy stubbornness, and to put ourselves, our Church, and our world, in God's hands, in the wounded and glorified Heart of Jesus—a Heart greater than all evil, greater than all our fears, greater than all our deserts and desires, greater than any of the victories of the past, the present, or the future.

---

8   Ps. 94 ESV; cf. Ps. 93 DRA.

21

In the Midst of Crisis, Be Driven by Faith, Not by Fear

I N OUR DAYS, WE ARE SEEING AN INTENSI-
fication of the spiritual battle as the situation within the
Catholic Church continues to deteriorate. Battles have casualties, and some of those casualties are Catholics who have lost
their faith or are tempted to leave the Church because of the
outrageous corruption, infidelity, and cowardice of its leaders and
the seeming lack of any coherent solution amidst anarchy.

The common denominator I have seen in those who are suffering
shipwreck is that they focus their attention primarily or even
exclusively on *the Church as a human institution*. By doing this, however,
we go at the whole thing backward.

The Church was not first in time, nor is it first in our lives.
Christ came first: *He* sought out the apostles, *He* attracted the
disciples, *He* redeemed us, *He* saves us even now, and the point
of our whole life is to get to know *Him*. To be sure, He is the
head of the Church, and we are members of that Church; it is
the "place" where we meet Him. But it is neither first nor last.

There is no way to know or understand or figure out the Church
(or theology or liturgy or anything) without that fundamental
relationship with Christ—being a son of the Father in and through
Him. He is the Rock below the rock (Peter/the pope), and He is
the only Rock that never shifts, being eternally stable.

We all know the scene in the Gospel where Jesus is sleeping
in the bow of the storm-tossed boat. To some people today, it
seems He's never going to wake up from His slumber. This, too,
is untrue. Rather, we are too busy freaking out to see that Christ
is already awake and *waiting to look us in the eye*, if only we would
stop for a moment, overcome our fear of silence, our fear of being
alone with Him, and rest in Him.

AMONG OTHER THINGS, HE IS ALIVE AND ACTIVE in the Eucharist. This is for real: praying before and living from the Eucharist has made great saints—in every century, in every region, in every conceivable situation. Who fixes God's Church? *Saints do.* How do men and women become saints? They do so by prayer and trust, not by thrashing around and venting and attacking.

Our modern vice *par excellence* is activism. We are all inveterate activists who think that it's "my fight for Catholicism" that matters. That is as sad as it is laughable. It is *righteous men*, however few they are, who hold this world together, as God said to Abraham. When Our Lady shows up, she doesn't say "Talk more" or "Kill 'em on Twitter!"; she says "Pray and do penance."

St. Augustine and St. Anselm, two of the greatest intellects and saints in our tradition, both held tightly to this saying from Isaiah: "Unless you believe, you will not understand." It may sound terribly anti-intellectual, but it's not a truth limited to the supernatural realm; the same truth is verified again and again in human relationships, too.

Understanding is not where we begin but where we end—when we have been faithful, when we have trusted, and when we have surrendered to a reality greater than ourselves and our ability to grasp it, or control it, or help it along.

WE ARE LIKE THE DISCIPLES IN THAT BOAT: WE expect Christ to do things according to *our* ideas of how it should be done: the warrior Messiah kicking the *viscera* out of the Romans. His idea of that strategy was shown clearly enough in Gethsemane and on Calvary, when He allowed Himself to be reduced to a bloody pulp, knowing that He was still in command and that He would have the last word, for He simply is the first and last and only Word. The Church lives His life and that means she lives His Passion: she, too—at least at times—will be a bloody mess, dying in her humiliation, but not left forever in that state.

Illustrations from history abound. The Arian crisis is often raised, and it should not be brushed aside, for it is enormously relevant to the problems we are facing. Someone who was born around the year 325 and who died around the year 400 would have spent his or her *entire life* under the shadow of Arianism, in a Church where the vast majority of bishops were heretics or cowards, where the few good bishops were hounded from place to place, where even popes were ineffectual or compromised. A pope excommunicated St. Athanasius, the greatest confessor of the age.

As Newman shows, it was the laity who kept the Faith. Did they complain that Jesus, the Son of God—the One whose royal divinity they confessed—was sleeping in their boat? Perhaps some did (and there is a way of complaining in the psalms that can be a form of prayer!), but the Faith survived because most of them didn't lose heart; they held fast, no matter what, knowing that it is not we who choose when we live, but Providence.

My hypothetical Catholic who lived from 325 to 400 sometimes had to worship out in the desert because the church buildings were stolen from the Catholics by the impostors. He admired the rare figures like St. Athanasius and St. Hilary, but he knew they were vastly outnumbered. That fourth-century Catholic never saw a healthy functional Church, either.

THE SITUATION IN REFORMATION ENGLAND WAS not too different for the Catholics who lived through it. A man who was born during Henry VIII's reign and who lived a long life would have seen his country go from Roman Catholicism to Anglo-Catholicism to Calvinism back to Catholicism and finally to Anglicanism. The politicians were complicit except for St. Thomas More; the bishops were complicit except for St. John Fisher.

Yet there were many great saints from that period, and many unsung heroes known to God alone, who were catapulted into holiness by the crisis. They were forced to seek refuge in Christ and not in princes, in mortal men in whom there is no help. Why did this happen? Why did He allow it to happen? We still do not have answers that can satisfy us in this life, but we can also see God's hand at work in the stupendous blossoms of sanctity that have graced England, including a renewal of martyrdoms worthy of the ancient Roman Empire.

It seems to me that many today are being driven by *fear*, including the fear of the dissolution of the "hierarchical" Church or its exposure as a fraud. This fear is generated, or at least made possible, by our inability to see the big picture, or by thinking that we see enough to know it's irrational and ugly. In any case, we want things to make sense on our own terms. That isn't how God does things—never has been, never will be. It's not for nothing that He is said to be infinite mystery. How could it be otherwise? He's not a giant creature lording it over us (as the serpent in the garden tried to get Adam and Eve to think). *He is the root of all. He is in everything and beyond everything.*

"It is not the task of Christianity to provide easy answers for every question, but to progressively make us aware of mystery. God is not so much the object of our knowledge as He is the cause of our awe," as Albert Rossi says. Rossi also makes the point, which I've come to rely on, that we need to learn to live with unclarity, uncertainty, ambiguity. One could even say it's a sign of mental health: the ability to go forward without seeing fully; the ability to let things be as they are, without despairing or hyperventilating; the ability to rest content with knowing what is essential. Rossi puts it in three statements: "I know that I don't know. I know that Christ knows. I trust Him."

THE FOUNDATION OF FRUITLESS SUFFERING IS THE lack of friendship with Jesus, just as the foundation of fruitful suffering is union with Him. We will not have, and cannot have, healthy relationships with anyone—including the Church and her leaders and her members—unless we have a relationship with Christ. To the extent that we do not have it, the inherent weakness, the tendency to dissipation in material and mortal things, will prevail.

When Our Lord puts us through a fiery trial, it is because He knows we need this; we need to *meet Him there.* A priest once said in the confessional: "The place where you are hurting is the place where Jesus wants to meet you. His wounds are your refuge: they have the power to heal your wounds." But they will not do so if we are busy fleeing Him, tearing out our hair, and questioning whether He loves us or cares about us. That is how we cut ourselves off from *the only place that reality is*, from the only One who sees it and governs it. The only way to have peace is to be in God's presence, because there is no peace outside of Him. Really: none at all. How could there be?

Our identity is not in being Catholic or in defending the Church but *in being Christ's* (that is what it means to be a "Christian"). Yes, we belong to His Body, but still our fundamental identity is to be His, to be a son in the Son, a beloved son of the Father. "This is my beloved Son, in whom I am well pleased." God says that to each one of us: You, *you* are my beloved son. There is no healing for wounded sonship and wounded fatherhood outside of the Father and the Son.

"Ask, and it will be given to you; seek, and you will find; knock, and it will be opened to you." Do we think the saints are liars? They asked, sought, and knocked, and they received, found, and got in—over and over again, for the past 2,000 years (or more, if we include the saints of the old covenant). We are lacking nothing that they had: we got the whole package. Yet we *do* have to ask, seek, and knock; it doesn't happen automatically or by chance. It happens by turning again and again to Him.

Our problems are usually *not* intellectual. They are problems of the heart, at the center of our being, not in the airy world of concepts, and therefore not in the realm of apologetics.

ONE PARTICULAR CAUSE OF PSYCHOLOGICAL UNREST today is the battleground of social media, the maelstrom of opinions from semi-educated loudmouths. Living in the midst of this realm can be frustrating and cause us to lose our peace (or to not be able to acquire it in the first place); it prioritizes the immediate, the egregious, and the depressing over the longer vision, the unmoving truth, the sparks of joy. We get buried alive in this avalanche of information. We suffocate from squadrons of pontificating pundits. Christians who find themselves in "panic mode," undergoing a personal crisis, have a moral obligation to pull back, to withdraw, or at least to restructure their approach to media.

I'm no paragon of virtue by any stretch of the imagination, but I would *die*—dry up spiritually—if I did not start my day at a distance from my online work. I've tried to erect barriers and boundaries to it. When I get up in the morning, before any device goes on, I pray Prime and read some Scripture; I go to Mass most days, and I take other breaks during the day to say Terce, Sext, or None (or all three if I can manage) so that I can maintain perspective and not lose my peace altogether—or lose my awareness of the one and only relationship that ultimately matters, the One on whom everything else depends.

Br. Lawrence of the Resurrection called it "the practice of the presence of God." I'm pretty clumsy at it, but I have enough experience to know that I would perish without it. This discipline of prayer and sacraments has kept me from losing my mind.

THAT IS THE CHALLENGE OF FAITH, IS IT NOT? Jesus says: *Come and see. Take up your cross and follow me. Seek first the kingdom of God and His righteousness, and all these other things will be added to you.* That's it: He invites, He does not compel. He promises everything to the one who gives himself to Him. The only way to know if He is right is to *do* it, to follow Him and to taste what He offers.

This is not a platitude but the Gospel truth. Sure, we can call it a leap of faith—but when you have ferocious beasts chasing you and you're running toward the edge, you're either going to have to leap into what you believe and hope to be God's embrace or lie down and let them consume you.

PRAYERS

FOR THE HOLY FATHER

℣. Oremus pro Pontifice nostro *N.*

℟. Dominus conservet eum, et vivificet eum, et beatum faciat eum in terra, et non tradat eum in animam inimicorum eius.

Pater Noster. Ave Maria.

Deus, omnium fidelium pastor et rector, famulum tuum *N.*, quem pastorem Ecclesiae tuae praeesse voluisti, propitius respice: da ei, quaesumus, verbo et exemplo, quibus praeest, proficere: ut ad vitam, una cum grege sibi credito, perveniat sempiternam. Per Christum Dominum nostrum. *Amen.*

. . . . .

℣. Let us pray for *N.*, our Pope.

℟. May the Lord preserve him, and give him life, and make him blessed upon the earth, and deliver him not up to the will of his enemies.

Our Father. Hail Mary.

O God, Shepherd and Ruler of all the faithful, look mercifully upon Thy servant *N.*, whom Thou hast willed to appoint shepherd over Thy Church: grant him, we beseech Thee, that by word and example he may profit those over whom he hath charge, so that, together with the flock committed to him, he may attain everlasting life. Through Christ our Lord. *Amen.*

FOR LOVERS OF TRADITION

O Lord, remember in Thy Kingdom *N.* and *N.*,
[names of individuals or communities]
and all religious, clergy, and laity throughout the world
who are dedicated or drawn to the *usus antiquior.*
Bless us, govern us, defend us, purify us, and multiply us
for the good of souls,
for the restoration of Thy Church,
and for the glory of Thy Holy Name.
Amen.

SELECT BIBLIOGRAPHY

The following bibliography does not list all the works cited throughout this book. Its purpose, rather, is to list works the author has
found especially helpful in furnishing background to, offering
illustrations of, or developing further the topics taken up in these
pages. It is the same as the bibliography included in volume 2.

ON THE PAPACY

Chamberlin, E. R. *The Bad Popes.* Dorchester: Dorset Press, 1994.

Chiron, Yves. *Pope Pius IX: The Man and the Myth.* Translated by Graham
Harrison. Kansas City, MO: Angelus Press, 2005.

———. *Saint Pius X: Restorer of the Church.* Translated by Graham Harrison.
Kansas City, MO: Angelus Press, 2002.

Cleenewerck, Laurent A. *His Broken Body: Understanding and Healing the Schism
between the Roman Catholic and Eastern Orthodox Churches.* Washington, DC:
Euclid University Consortium Press, 2007.

Coulombe, Charles A. *Vicars of Christ: A History of the Popes.* Arcadia, CA:
Tumblar House, 2014.

da Silveira, Arnaldo Vidigal Xavier. *Can Documents of the Magisterium of the
Church Contain Errors? Can the Catholic Faithful Resist Them?* Translated by
John R. Spann and José A. Schelini. Spring Grove, PA: The American
Society for the Defense of Tradition, Family and Property, 2015.

———. *Can a Pope Be . . . a Heretic? The Theological Hypothesis of a Heretical Pope.*
Translated by John Spann. Porto: Caminhos Romanos, 2018.

de Mattei, Roberto. *Love for the Papacy and Filial Resistance to the Pope in the
History of the Church.* Brooklyn, NY: Angelico Press, 2019.

———. *Saint Pius V.* Translated by Giuseppe Pellegrino. Manchester, NH:
Sophia Institute Press, 2021.

Hull, Geoffrey. *The Banished Heart: Origins of Heteropraxis in the Catholic
Church.* London/New York: T&T Clark, 2010.

Journet, Charles. *The Church of the Word Incarnate: An Essay in Speculative
Theology.* Translated by A.H.C. Downes. Volume 1: The Apostolic
Hierarchy. London/New York: Sheed and Ward, 1955.

———. *The Theology of the Church.* Translated by Victor Szczurek, O.Praem.
San Francisco: Ignatius Press, 2004.

Joy, John. *On the Ordinary and Extraordinary Magisterium from Joseph Kleutgen to
the Second Vatican Council.* Studia Oecumenica Friburgensia 84. Münster:
Aschendorff Verlag, 2017.

Kwasniewski, Peter A., ed. *Are Canonizations Infallible? Revisiting a Disputed
Question.* Waterloo, ON: Arouca Press, 2021.

McCaffrey, Neil. *And Rightly So: Selected Letters and Articles of Neil McCaffrey.* Edited by Peter A. Kwasniewski. Fort Collins, CO: Roman Catholic Books, 2019. [The second section, "Reformation and Deformation in the Catholic Church," 135–220, contains penetrating observations on the postconciliar popes and especially on the liturgical reform.]

Mosebach, Martin. *Subversive Catholicism: Papacy, Liturgy, Church.* Translated by Sebastian Condon and Graham Harrison. Brooklyn: Angelico Press, 2019.

Ratzinger, Joseph. *Called to Communion: Understanding the Church Today.* Translated by Adrian Walker. San Francisco: Ignatius Press, 1996.

Siecienski, A. Edward. *The Papacy and the Orthodox. Sources and History of a Debate.* New York: Oxford University Press, 2017.

ON POPE FRANCIS

Borghesi, Massimo. *The Mind of Pope Francis: Jorge Mario Bergoglio's Intellectual Journey.* Translated by Barry Hudock. Collegeville, MN: Liturgical Press Academic, 2018.

de Valladares, Martha Alegría Reichmann. *Sacred Betrayals: A Widow Raises Her Voice against the Corruption of the Francis Papacy.* Translated by Matthew Cullinan Hoffman. Front Royal, VA: Faithful Insight Books, 2021.

Douthat, Ross. *To Change the Church: Pope Francis and the Future of Catholicism.* New York: Simon & Schuster, 2018.

Faggioli, Massimo. *The Liminal Papacy of Pope Francis: Moving Toward Global Catholicity.* Maryknoll, NY: Orbis Books, 2020.

Lamont, John R.T. and Claudio Pierantoni, eds. *Defending the Faith against Present Heresies.* Waterloo, ON: Arouca Press, 2021.

Lanzetta, Serafino M. *The Symphony of Truth: Theological Essays.* Waterloo, ON: Arouca Press, 2021.

Lawler, Philip F. *Lost Shepherd: How Pope Francis Is Misleading His Flock.* Washington, DC: Regnery Gateway, 2018.

Lee, Brian Y., and Thomas L. Knoebel, eds. *Discovering Pope Francis: The Roots of Jorge Mario Bergoglio's Thinking.* Collegeville, MN: Liturgical Press Academic, 2019.

Meloni, Julia. *The St. Gallen Mafia: Exposing the Secret Reform Group within the Church.* Gastonia, NC: TAN Books, 2021.

Neumayr, George. *The Political Pope: How Pope Francis Is Delighting the Liberal Left and Abandoning Conservatives.* New York: Hachette Book Group, 2017.

Sire, Henry. *The Dictator Pope: The Inside Story of the Francis Papacy.* Washington, DC: Regnery Publishing, 2018.

Ureta, José Antonio. *Pope Francis's "Paradigm Shift": Continuity or Rupture in the Mission of the Church?* Translated by José A. Schelini. Spring Grove, PA: The American Society for the Defense of Tradition, Family and Property, 2018.

Yiannopoulos, Milo. *Diabolical: How Pope Francis Has Betrayed Clerical Abuse Victims Like Me—and Why He Has To Go.* New York: Bombardier Books, 2018.

MODERN CHURCH HISTORY AND CONTROVERSY

Amerio, Romano. *Iota Unum: A Study of Changes in the Catholic Church in the XXth Century*. Trans. John P. Parsons. Kansas City: Sarto House, 1996.

Buck, Roger. *Cor Jesu Sacratissimum: From Secularism and the New Age to Christendom Renewed*. Kettering, OH: Angelico Press, 2016.

de Mattei, Roberto. *Apologia for Tradition. A Defense of Tradition Grounded in the Historical Context of the Faith*. Translated by Michael J. Miller. Kansas City, MO: Angelus Press, 2019.

——. *The Second Vatican Council: An Unwritten Story*. Translated by Patrick T. Brannan, S.J., Michael J. Miller, and Kenneth D. Whitehead. Edited by Michael J. Miller. Fitzwilliam, NH: Loreto Publications, 2012.

Ferrara, Christopher, and Thomas Woods. *The Great Façade: The Regime of Novelty in the Catholic Church from Vatican II to the Francis Revolution*. Second ed. Kettering, OH: Angelico Press, 2015.

Feser, Edward, and Joseph Bessette. *By Man Shall His Blood Be Shed: A Catholic Defense of Capital Punishment*. San Francisco: Ignatius Press, 2017.

Guimarães, Atila Sinke, Michael J. Matt, John Vennari, Marian Therese Horvat. *We Resist You to the Face*. Los Angeles: Tradition In Action, 2000.

Haynes, Michael. *A Catechism of Errors: A Critique of the Principal Errors of the Catechism of the Catholic Church*. Fitzwilliam, NH: Loreto Publications, 2021.

Lawler, Philip F. *The Smoke of Satan: How Corrupt and Cowardly Bishops Betrayed Christ, His Church, and the Faithful . . . and What Can Be Done About It*. Charlotte, NC: TAN Books, 2018.

Malloy, Christopher J. *False Mercy: Recent Heresies Distorting Catholic Truth*. Manchester, NH: Sophia Institute Press, 2021.

McGinley, Brandon. *The Prodigal Church: Restoring Catholic Tradition in an Age of Deception*. Manchester, NH: Sophia Institute Press, 2020.

Muggeridge, Anne Roche. *The Desolate City: Revolution in the Catholic Church*. Revised and expanded. New York: HarperCollins, 1990.

Murr, Charles Theodore. *The Godmother: Madre Pascalina, A Feminine Tour de Force*. N.p.: Independently published, 2017.

——. *Murder in the 33rd Degree: The Gagnon Investigation into Vatican Freemasonry*. N.p.: Independently published, 2022.

Sammons, Eric. *Deadly Indifference: How the Church Lost Her Mission and How We Can Reclaim It*. Manchester, NH: Crisis Publications, 2021.

Schneider, Most Rev. Athanasius, and Diane Montagna. *Christus Vincit. Christ's Triumph Over the Darkness of the Age*. Brooklyn, NY: Angelico Press, 2019.

Sire, H.J.A. [Henry]. *Phoenix from the Ashes: The Making, Unmaking, and Restoration of Catholic Tradition*. Kettering, OH: Angelico Press, 2015.

Trower, Philip. *The Catholic Church and the Counter-faith: A Study of the Roots of Modern Secularism, Relativism and de-Christianisation*. Oxford: Family Publications, 2006.

———. *Turmoil and Truth: The Historical Roots of the Modern Crisis in the Catholic Church*. Oxford: Family Publications and San Francisco: Ignatius Press, 2003.

Valli, Aldo Maria and Aurelio Porfiri. *Uprooted: Dialogues on the Liquid Church*. Translated by Giuseppe Pellegrino. Hong Kong: Chorabooks, 2019.

ON LITURGICAL QUESTIONS

Casini, Tito. *The Torn Tunic. Letter of a Catholic on the "Liturgical Reform."* Originally published by Fidelity Books in 1967; repr. Brooklyn, NY: Angelico Press, 2020.

Cekada, Anthony. *Work of Human Hands: A Theological Critique of the Mass of Paul VI*. West Chester, OH: Philothea Press, 2010.

Chiron, Yves. *Annibale Bugnini, Reformer of the Liturgy*. Translated by John Pepino. Brooklyn, NY: Angelico Press, 2018.

Davies, Michael. *Cranmer's Godly Order: The Destruction of Catholicism through Liturgical Change*. Fort Collins, CO: Roman Catholic Books, 1995.

———. *Pope Paul's New Mass*. Kansas City, MO: Angelus Press, 2009.

Dulac, Raymond. *In Defence of the Roman Mass*. Translated by Peadar Walsh. N.p.: Te Deum Press, 2020.

Fiedrowicz, Michael. *The Traditional Mass: History, Form, and Theology of the Classical Roman Rite*. Translated by Rose Pfeifer. Brooklyn, NY: Angelico Press, 2020.

Kwasniewski, Peter A., ed. *From Benedict's Peace to Francis's War: Catholics Respond to the Motu Proprio* Traditionis Custodes *on the Latin Mass*. Brooklyn, NY: Angelico Press, 2021.

———. *Holy Bread of Eternal Life: Restoring Eucharistic Reverence in an Age of Impiety*. Manchester, NH: Sophia Institute Press, 2020.

———. *Ministers of Christ: Recovering the Roles of Clergy and Laity in an Age of Confusion*. Manchester, NH: Crisis Publications, 2021.

———. *Noble Beauty, Transcendent Holiness: Why the Modern Age Needs the Mass of Ages*. Kettering, OH: Angelico Press, 2017.

———. *Reclaiming Our Roman Catholic Birthright: The Genius and Timeliness of the Traditional Latin Mass*. Brooklyn, NY: Angelico Press, 2020.

———. *Resurgent in the Midst of Crisis: Sacred Liturgy, the Traditional Latin Mass, and Renewal in the Church*. Kettering, OH: Angelico Press, 2014.

———. *Tradition and Sanity: Conversations and Dialogues of a Postconciliar Exile*. Brooklyn, NY: Angelico Press, 2018.

———. *True Obedience in the Church: A Guide to Discernment in Challenging Times*. Manchester, NH: Sophia Institute Press, 2021.

Mosebach, Martin. *The Heresy of Formlessness: The Roman Liturgy and Its Enemy*. Revised and expanded edition. Translated by Graham Harrison. Brooklyn, NY: Angelico Press, 2018.

INDEX OF NAMES
AND SUBJECTS
(for Volume 1)

ABOUT THE AUTHOR

Peter A. Kwasniewski holds a B.A. in Liberal Arts from Thomas Aquinas College and an M.A. and Ph.D. in Philosophy from the Catholic University of America, with a specialization in the thought of St. Thomas Aquinas. After teaching at the International Theological Institute in Austria from 1999–2006, he joined the founding team of Wyoming Catholic College, where he taught theology, philosophy, music, and art history and directed the choir and schola until 2018. Today, he is a full-time writer and speaker whose work is seen at websites and in periodicals such as *New Liturgical Movement, OnePeterFive, Rorate Caeli, The Remnant, Catholic Family News,* and *Latin Mass Magazine.* Dr. Kwasniewski has published extensively in academic and popular venues on sacramental and liturgical theology, the history and aesthetics of music, Catholic Social Teaching, and issues in the modern Church. He has written or edited many books and his work has been translated into at least eighteen languages. For more information, visit his website: www.peterkwasniewski.com.

Lightning Source UK Ltd.
Milton Keynes UK
UKHW012007070722
405551UK00010B/200/J